great
TUNISIAN CROCHET
projects

Kristel Salgarollo

STACKPOLE
BOOKS
Guilford, Connecticut

Contents

THE PROJECTS

Introduction

My grandmother was an independent and creative woman, passionate about fiber crafts. Always living hand-to-mouth, she used and reused everything she could, always succeeding in creating something out of nothing. In fact, she had a good head for recycling long before today's "upcycling" trend, and a certain disposition toward a style that was . . . let's say "colorful"!

I still have a photo of her dressed in one of her crocheted dresses, for which she had used more than a hundred yarns in different colors. Sitting on her couch, surrounded by pillows that were themselves multicolored, our dear Mien (pronounced "meen") almost blends into the background! I must add that her house was just like Pippi Longstocking's. In particular, I remember a rug crocheted from nylon stockings, surprisingly sturdy, but which our kids' eyes found bizarre at least. I deeply regret today that I don't have anything saved from that extravagant universe, which would be all the rage now that vintage and handmade things are in fashion!

As the adage says, "the apple doesn't fall far from the tree," and of her three granddaughters (my sisters and myself), two share the same love for fiber arts, even earning their living from them (my youngest sister, Inez, named her shop after our Mien, by the way), and the third one paints. One of her great-granddaughters has also inherited the same uncontrolled taste for couture, and it's likely that she will take up the torch after her aunts.

This all started very early for me. I was just six years old when I caught a glimpse of everything that was possible with a simple crochet hook, thanks to a classmate and her extraordinary lilac and mint green pullover that I couldn't take my eyes off. Despite my fascination with these crocheted motifs, I was not excited by the sewing classes at school; the projects we made seemed boring to me.

The change came in my adolescent years. At fourteen, I started to crochet all sorts of tunics for myself and my friends. I worked without a pattern, following my own inspiration, a bit "à la Mien." But who would have been surprised at that at the beginning of the 1970s, at the height of "flower power"?

During my last year of high school, I made a whole afghan of granny squares during my math class—contrary to what I'd believed earlier, school was finally supporting my progress in the fiber arts. Sitting in the back row, I crocheted secretly in my lap. I don't need to tell you that my end-of-the-year exams were not great, leading my teacher, Monsieur Van den Bossche, to say that I would never go far in life.

He would certainly be happy to learn that with the little knowledge of logarithms and integrals that he managed to transmit to me despite myself, I have succeeded in making something of my existence.

Many among you know me thanks to the patchwork I discovered later on. You now know everything (or almost everything) about how I took up crocheting, which I have never put down since. I always have a project in progress, which I bring with me in the car, on the train, or in the waiting rooms that have now replaced math class! This is one of the great advantages and pleasures of this craft.

Six years ago, when I decided to expand my shop to offer wool and cotton yarns in addition to quilting fabrics, I never dreamed that knitting and crocheting would experience such a resurgence in popularity that they would break out of the little circle they had occupied and steal the hearts of so many young mothers and hip young women.

I am not yet a grandmother, and I'm no longer a young mother. My three sons have left home, and each one of them can curl up in one of my crocheted afghans. Now I can't wait to spoil grandchildren. There are so many beautiful things to make for little ones! I plan to keep on with it for a long time, with the quilting as well as the crocheting (and all the rest!); I'm not running out of ideas, and I already have enough to keep me busy for the next hundred years!

I'm thrilled to share this bit of personal history with you, and I hope you get a lot of enjoyment from making the projects in this book. To finish, I'd like to extend a big thank-you to Martine and Chantal.

Kristel Salgarollo

Technique Basics

BASIC CROCHET STITCHES

⬭ Chain (ch)

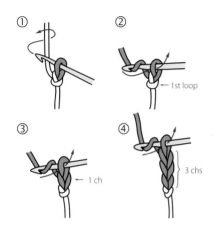

1. Wrap the yarn around the crochet hook (yarn over) in the direction indicated by the arrow.

2. Pull the yarn up through the base loop to form the first chain stitch.

3. Pull up another yarn over to form the second chain stitch.

4. Repeat the process as many times as needed.

⬭ Slip Stitch (Sl st)

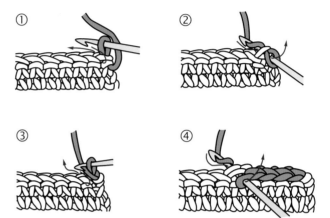

1. At the end of the row, insert the hook directly into the first stitch, as shown by the arrow.

2. Yarn over, then pull the yarn through to the front, following the arrow.

3. Insert the hook into the next stitch as shown by the arrow.

4. This stitch has a tendency to get very tight, so it's recommended that you work loosely (stretching out the stitches a bit as you go).

☒ Single Crochet (sc)

1. Chain 1, turn the work, then insert the hook as shown in the diagram.

2. Yarn over and draw the yarn through the stitch, following the arrow.

3. Yarn over and draw the yarn through both loops on the hook.

4. The single crochet is completed. Insert the hook again as shown in step 1 and then continue through steps 2 and 3 to make another single crochet.

5. Here 3 single crochets have been completed.

Double Crochet (dc)

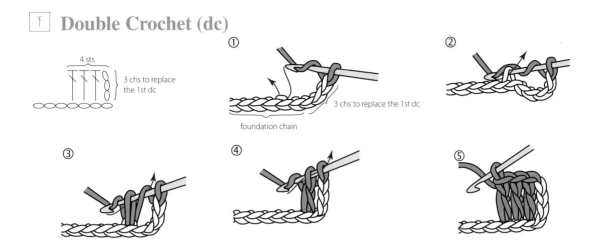

1. Start by working 3 chain stitches that count as the first double crochet. Next, yarn over, then insert the hook on the right side, indicated in the diagram by an arrow.

2. Yarn over and draw the yarn through the stitch, following the arrow.

3. Yarn over and draw the yarn through the next 2 loops on the hook.

4. Yarn over and draw the yarn through the remaining 2 loops on the hook.

5. Yarn over and insert the hook as in step 1, then repeat steps 2 to 4 to complete another double crochet. Here we have 4 double crochets (that is, 3 chains which stand in for the first double crochet, and 3 double crochets).

BASICS OF TUNISIAN CROCHET

Unlike traditional crochet, Tunisian crochet (also known as the afghan stitch) is always worked from the right side of the piece. This technique consists of a forward pass, in which all the stitches are kept on the hook, and a return pass, where the stitches are bound off. For this reason, you need a long hook with a stopper at the end to hold the stitches on.

The typical Tunisian crochet hook is about 11¾ in. (30 cm) long. It is perfect for making scarves, pillows, and other projects that aren't too big; on the other hand, it is too small to crochet an afghan with. For larger projects, there is a special kind of hook with a flexible extension with a stopper at the end, a little like circular knitting needles. This special hook allows you to work all the way across an afghan. This type of crochet hook is available from different brands (for specifics, search online).

Even though Tunisian crochet is always worked on the right side of the piece, there is clearly a right side and a wrong side (which looks like the wrong side of a knitted piece). The wrong side can also be decorative. The **forward pass** is worked from right to left, keeping all the stitches on the hook as you go. At the end of the pass, you have all the stitches on the hook. The **return pass** is worked from left to right, binding off the stitches as you go. At the end of the pass, there is only one loop left on the hook.

You should note that this technique has a tendency to produce rigid work; this is why it's preferable to use a larger crochet hook than recommended on the yarn label. So, for example, for a yarn that recommends a G-5 (4 mm) crochet hook, use an H-8 (5 mm) hook.

①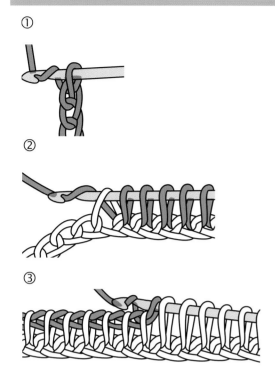

1. Work a foundation chain.

2. First forward pass (right to left): Insert the hook into the 2nd chain from the hook, *yarn over, draw the yarn through the stitch to pull up a loop. Leave the loop on the hook.* Repeat from * to * across, with each chain of the foundation chain.

②

3. Return pass (left to right): DO NOT TURN THE WORK; yarn over, draw the yarn through the first loop on the hook. *Yarn over, draw through 2 loops*; repeat from * to * across the row. At the end of the row, 1 loop remains on the hook.

Note: Except for when you are assembling parts of a project, always work every return pass in this way.

③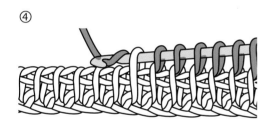

4. Forward pass (and all following forward passes): Insert the hook behind the 2nd vertical bar of the previous forward pass, yarn over, pull up a loop, *insert the hook behind the next vertical bar, yarn over, and pull up a loop (1 Tunisian simple stitch)*; repeat from * to * all the way across the row.

Note: Certain methods start the row with 1 chain, but I never do this because the edge of the work looks much nicer without this extra stitch.

④

5. Finishing row (on a forward pass): To keep the work from stretching or warping, crochet a row of single crochets: Chain 1, then work 1 single crochet in each vertical bar of the previous forward pass.

⑤

This technique translates into a diagram format as follows:

Diagram of basic stitches

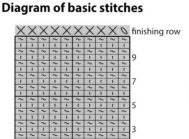

finishing row

| | Tunisian simple stitch: Insert the hook behind the vertical bar, yarn over, pull up a loop.

| ~ | Return: Yarn over, pull through 1 loop, then repeat *yarn over, pull through 2 loops* across the row.

Repeat the part inside the box.

∘ Chain (ch): Yarn over, then pull the yarn through the loop.

× Single crochet (sc): Insert the hook into the next stitch, yarn over and pull up a loop, then yarn over and pull through all the loops on the hook.

TUNISIAN CROCHET BLOCKS

It's possible to crochet blocks with Tunisian crochet. It's not as easy as straight rows, but once you've become familiar with the technique, the possibilities are infinite!

Note: If the blocks aren't too big, you can use a regular crochet hook.

Adding Blocks in a Row

For blocks in a row, you need to start with a foundation chain of a length that is a multiple of the number of stitches per block. Or for a block that isn't necessarily square, you must add the number of stitches on the base of the block to the total number of rows, including the finishing row (since with this technique, the chains of the foundation chain serve as two sides of the block). For example, for a block of 8 base stitches and 7 rows, you should crochet 8 + 7 = 15 chains. Thus, if you want to crochet 8 blocks, each using 15 chains, your foundation chain should be 8 x 15 stitches long, that is 120 chains.

Tip: To be safe, always chain more stitches than you need; it's easier to undo unneeded stitches than to have to add extra stitches!

The following step-by-step instructions correspond to the example of 15-stitch blocks.

1. Work a foundation chain of the required length (adding a few extra chains for safety).

2. First row (forward and return passes):
Forward pass: Repeat the following 7 times: *Insert the hook into a stitch, yarn over, and bring the yarn through the stitch,* starting from the second chain from the hook. You should have 8 loops on the hook.

Return pass: Repeat the following 7 times: *Yarn over, pull through 2 loops.* You will have 8 vertical bars.

*Note: Unlike with the basic stitch (steps 3 to 6), the return pass for blocks worked in a row does not begin with *yarn over, pull through the first loop,* but with a yarn over pulled through the first 2 loops on the hook.*

3. Second row:
Forward pass: Repeat the following 7 times: *Insert the hook behind the vertical bar of the first stitch in the previous row, yarn over, and pull the yarn up*, skip 1 stitch on the foundation chain (corner of block), insert the hook into the next stitch (see the arrow on the diagram), yarn over, and pull up a loop. You should have 8 loops on the hook.

Insert the hook into the second chain.

Return pass: Work as for the first row.

4. Third row:
Forward pass: Repeat the following 7 times: *Insert the hook behind the vertical bar of the first stitch in the previous row, yarn over, and pull up a loop,* insert the hook into the next stitch of the foundation chain, yarn over, pull up a loop (see diagram). You should have 8 loops on the hook.

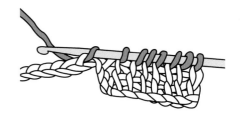

Return pass: Work as for the first row.

5. Fourth, fifth, and sixth rows:
Work as for Row 3 (forward and return passes).

6. **Seventh row/finishing row for the block:**
Chain 1, repeat the following 6 times: *Insert the hook behind the vertical bar of the first stitch in the previous row, yarn over, pull up a loop, then yarn over and pull through both loops (1 sc).* Work 1 Sl st in the next st of the foundation chain.

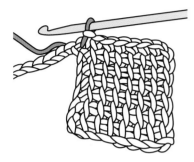

Work the other blocks following the same pattern.

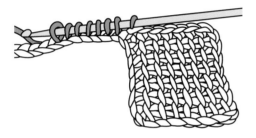

This technique translates into a chart as follows:

Chart

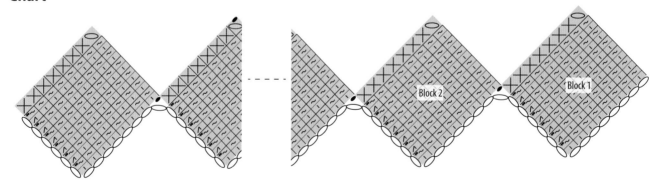

| | Tunisian simple stitch: Insert the hook behind the vertical bar, yarn over, pull up a loop.

~ **Return:** Yarn over, draw through 2 loops.

∧ Insert the hook into the corresponding stitch of the neighboring block, yarn over, pull up a loop.

*~ **Assembly return:** Repeat *yarn over, draw through 2 loops* across the row.

○ **Chain (ch):** Yarn over, draw the yarn through the loop on the hook.

● **Slip stitch (Sl st):** Insert the hook into a stitch, yarn over, and draw the yarn through the stitch and the loop on the hook.

× **Single crochet (sc):** Insert the hook into a stitch, yarn over and pull up a loop, yarn over and draw the yarn through all the loops on the hook.

Adding Blocks Diagonally

In this case, the first block is crocheted separately, then the others are crocheted and attached to the previous blocks as you go.

1. For Block 1 (bottom left corner): Work a chain for the base of this block only (for example, ch 8), then crochet 6 rows (forward and return passes) in Tunisian simple stitch, and work the finishing row. Cut the yarn.

2. For Block 2 (to the left of Block 1): Attach the yarn to the end of the base chain of the previous block and work a base chain of 7 sts (see illustration 1); repeat the following 6 times: *Insert the hook into the next stitch, yarn over, pull up a loop,* starting from the second chain from the hook, then attach the block to the previous block by inserting the hook in the corresponding stitch of the first row on the bottom right and pulling up a loop. You should have 8 loops on the hook (see illustration 2). For the return pass, repeat *yarn over, draw through 2 loops* across the whole row. Work a total of 6 rows (forward and return passes) following this pattern; that is, attaching the block to the previous block as you go, and finish with 1 row of single crochet and a slip stitch in the corresponding stitch of Block 1.

This technique translates into chart form as follows:

Chart

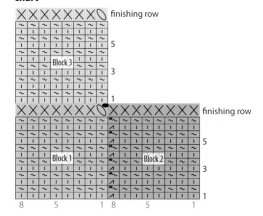

| Tunisian simple stitch: Insert the hook behind the vertical bar, yarn over, pull up a loop.

~ Return: Yarn over, draw through 1 loop (first stitch on non-assembly rows), then repeat *yarn over, draw through 2 loops* across the row.

⟋ Insert the hook into the corresponding stitch of the neighboring block, yarn over, pull up a loop.

*~ Assembly return: Repeat *yarn over, draw through 2 loops* across the row.

⊙ Chain (ch): Yarn over, draw the yarn through the loop on the hook.

● Slip stitch (Sl st): Insert the hook into a stitch, yarn over, and draw the yarn through the stitch and the loop on the hook.

× Single crochet (sc): Insert the hook into a stitch, yarn over and pull up a loop, yarn over and draw the yarn through all the loops on the hook.

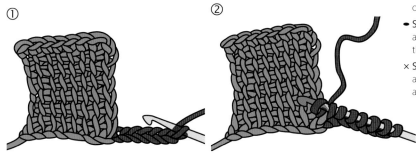

① ②

3. For Block 3 (on top of Block 1): Attach the yarn and pick up 8 loops in the stitches of the last row of Block 1, then work as for Block 1.

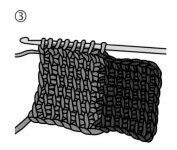

③

Note: With this technique, you can change color on each block, which requires cutting the yarn at the end of each block. However, you can also work Block 1 in one color and Blocks 2 and 3 in another. In this case, don't cut the yarn at the end of Block 2, but continue directly with Block 3.

MAKING A PILLOW COVER

1. Carefully measure the dimensions of the piece.

2. From fabric, cut out the following pieces (adding seam allowances):

1 x the dimensions + 4 in. (10 cm) = front (*a*)

$^1/_3$ x *a* + $^3/_4$ in. (2 cm) = back (*b*)

Note*: The $^3/_4$ in. (2 cm) is intended for a hem.*

$^2/_3$ x *a* + 2 in. (5 cm) + $^3/_4$ in. (2 cm) = back (*c*)

Note*: The 2 in. (5 cm) allows the two half-backs to overlap each other. Adapt this measurement according to the size of your pillow cover: The larger the piece, the more important the overlap is.*

Make a hem on the wrong side of the edges of the two back pieces that will overlap. Overstitch the hem. With right sides together, put the front of the pillow cover and the backs together, overlapping the flaps. Baste the two flaps together to hold the fabric in place, then sew all the way around the edge of the cover. Notch the corners, remove the basting stitches, and turn the piece right-side out. Sew the crocheted piece on the front with blind stitch. Put the pillow inside the cover using the opening between the flaps.

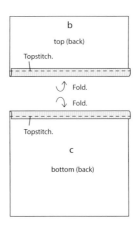

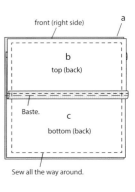

MAKING FRINGE

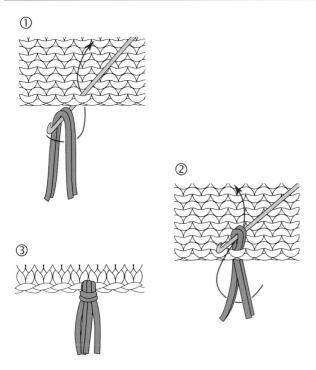

1. Prepare as many strands of yarn as needed for the fringe. Then, working on the wrong side of the work, insert the hook into the desired stitch and use it to pull the strands of fringe through this stitch. This forms a loop made from the fringe strands.

2. Use the crochet hook to pull all the ends of the fringe through the loop (see the arrow).

3. On the right side of the work, one bundle of fringe is now finished.

MAKING A POM-POM

 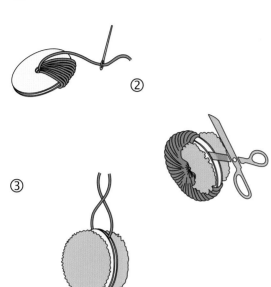

Prepare two circles of cardboard of the desired size. Make a hole in the center.

1. Place the two cardboard templates together, one on top of the other, then use a yarn needle to pass the yarn through the central hole of the two templates until the circles are full.

2. Slide the point of the scissors under the strands of yarn, in between the two templates. Cut the strands of yarn all the way around the outer edge.

3. Slip a strand of yarn between the two cardboard pieces. Pull tight and tie a double knot. Remove the cardboard pieces. Use the scissors to shape the pom-pom and even out the length of the strands.

ABBREVIATIONS

ch(s)	chain
dc	double crochet
hdc	half double crochet
rnd(s)	round(s)
sc	single crochet
Sl st	slip stitch
st(s)	stitch(es)
tr	treble crochet
Tss	Tunisian simple stitch

A NOTE ON SIZING

In this book, the dimensions are given purely as a guide. In fact, the finished pieces will have different sizes, depending on your choice of yarns, the size of hook you use, and how tightly you crochet (which differs from one person to another).

For this reason, the amount of fabric to make a lining or a pillow cover, for example, is never given precisely, since it depends on the size of the finished piece.

However, to achieve finished projects of the sizes given in the book, you can begin by working a gauge swatch with your chosen hook and adapting the instructions given as needed according to the swatch obtained.

Afghans
and More

Balloon Flight

Finished Measurements

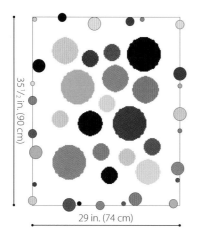

35 1/2 in. (90 cm)

29 in. (74 cm)

Materials

- 12.3 oz./350 g #3 DK weight wool yarn in Main Color (shown in white; Rowan Pure Wool DK; 100% wool; 1.76 oz./50 g, 142 yd./130 m per ball)
- 1.76 oz./50 g #3 DK weight wool in each of 8 colors of your choice
- Enough fabric to line the piece
- Size G-6 (4.0 mm) Tunisian crochet hook, extra long (or one size larger than the recommended size for the yarn)

Stitches Used

Tunisian simple stitch (see page 6)
Chain (ch), slip stitch (Sl st), and double crochet (dc) (see pages 4–5)

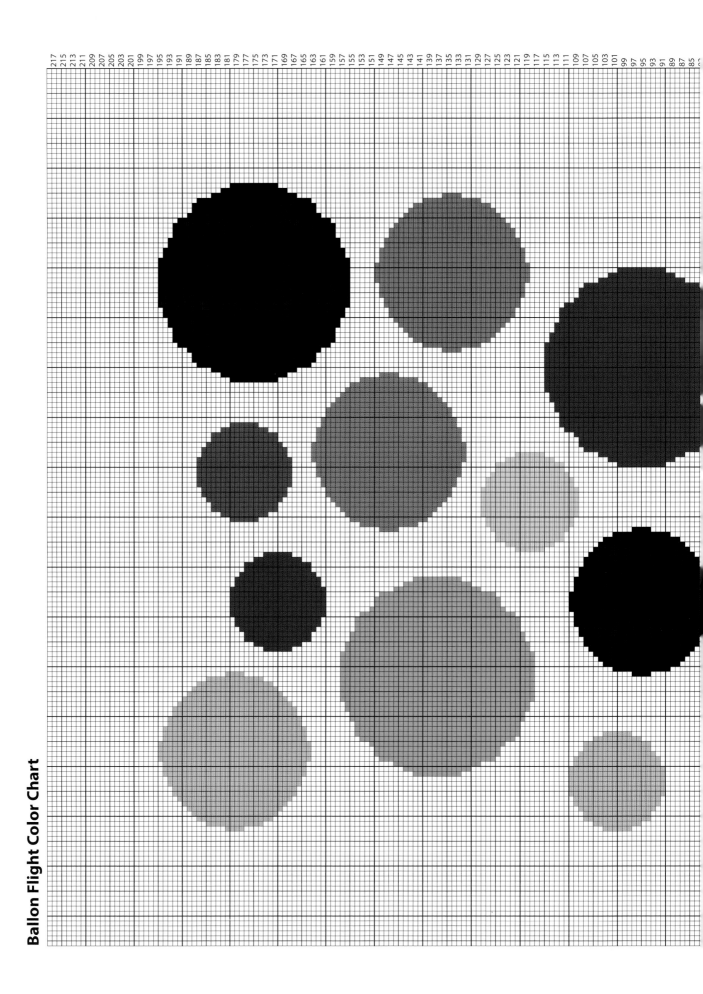

Ballon Flight Color Chart

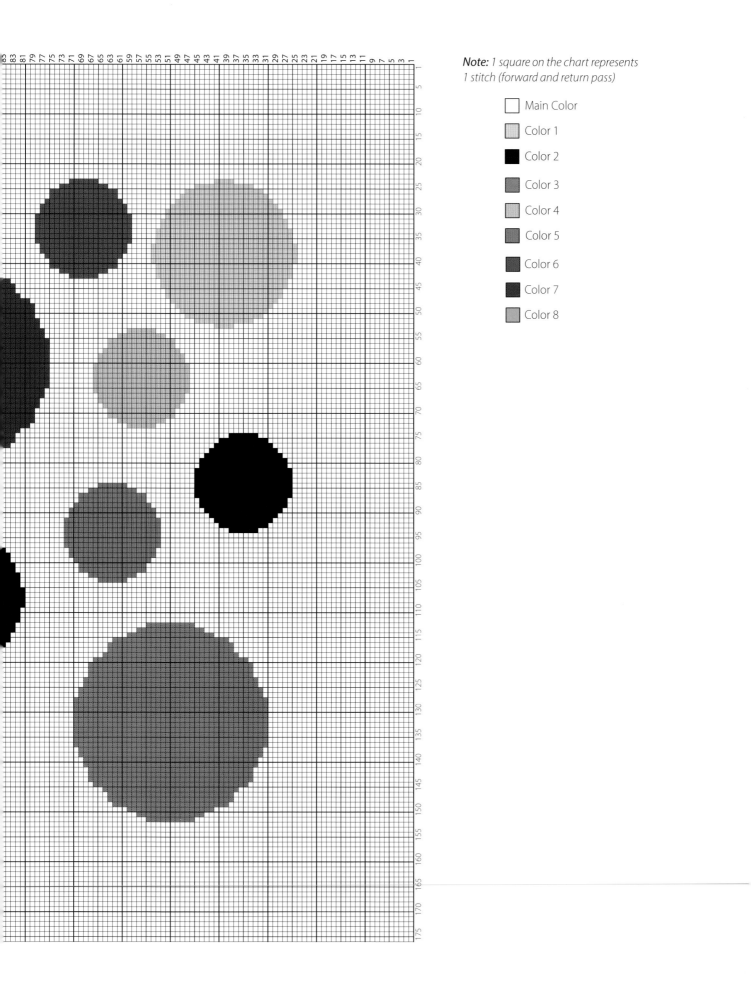

Balloon Flight

Instructions

With the Main Color, work a foundation chain of 176 stitches, then work 23 rows in Tunisian simple stitch. Continue, changing colors as shown in the chart on pages 16 and 17, then work 23 more rows in Main Color. Be sure to finish with the finishing row (see page 6). Fasten off and weave in the ends.

Note: When you change colors, cross the yarns over one another, as for intarsia knitting.

Small, Medium, and Large Decorative Circles

Start with a ring of 6 chs, close with a Sl st, then work the round(s) shown in the diagrams below. Fasten off and weave in the ends. Crochet 3 sizes of circle in each color (except Main Color).

Small Circle

Medium Circle

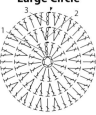

Large Circle

◀ Fasten off.

◯ **Chain (ch):** Yarn over, draw the yarn through the loop on the hook.

● **Slip stitch (Sl st):** Insert the hook into a stitch, yarn over, and draw the yarn through the stitch and the loop on the hook.

┬ **Double crochet (dc):** Yarn over, then insert the hook into the stitch, yarn over and pull up a loop, then work *yarn over, pull through 2 loops* twice.

Finishing

Sew the circles around the edges of the afghan, positioning some halfway over the edge (see photo). Line the afghan with fabric.

Bayadère

Bayadère

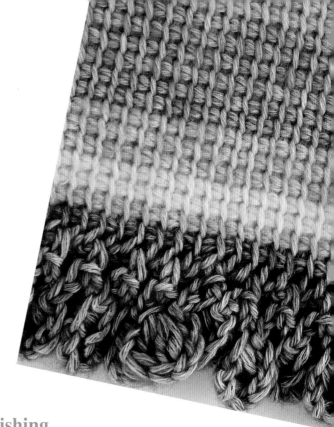

Finished Measurements

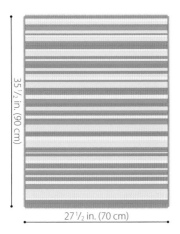

35 1/2 in. (90 cm)

27 1/2 in. (70 cm)

Materials

- 3.5 oz./100 g #2 fine weight yarn in each of 6 coordinating colors of your choice, plus 3.5 oz./100 g extra of 1 of these colors for the edging (shown in Scheepjeswol Stone Washed; 78% cotton, 22% acrylic; 1.76 oz./50 g, 142 yd./130 m per skein)
- Size G-6 (4.0 mm) extra-long Tunisian crochet hook (or one size larger than the recommended size for the yarn)

Stitches Used

Tunisian simple stitch (see page 6)
Chain (ch), slip stitch (Sl st), single crochet (sc)
   (see pages 4–5)
Popcorn stitch (see chart key)

Instructions

Start with a foundation chain of 160 sts (which should be about 27 1/2 in. (70 cm)—if this is not the case, adjust the number of stitches to obtain this size). Work in Tunisian simple stitch, changing colors as shown in the chart on page 21. After the stripes have been worked, the piece should measure about 35 1/2 in. (90 cm) long (if this is not the case, adjust by crocheting more or fewer stripes). Finish with a finishing row (see page 6).

Note: To add stripes, randomly vary the number of rows and the colors used.

Finishing

Crochet the edging as follows:
   Round 1: With chosen yarn, work 1 round of sc in each st around, close the round with a Sl st (see chart).
   Round 2: Work as shown in the chart. Close the round with a Sl st and fasten off. Weave in all ends.

Edging

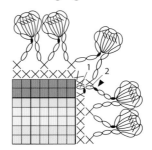

◀ Fasten off.

⊝ **Chain (ch):** Yarn over, draw the yarn through the loop on the hook.

● **Slip stitch (Sl st):** Insert the hook into a stitch, yarn over, and draw the yarn through the stitch and the loop on the hook.

× **Single crochet (sc):** Insert the hook into a stitch, yarn over and pull up a loop, yarn over and draw the yarn through all the loops on the hook.

† **Double crochet (dc):** Yarn over, then insert the hook into the stitch, yarn over and pull up a loop, then work *yarn over, pull through 2 loops* twice.

⬥ **5-double crochet popcorn stitch:** Work 5 double crochets, then stretch out the loop on the hook; remove the hook and insert the hook through the top of the first of the 5 double crochets, pick up the dropped loop again and pull it through this stitch. Tighten the loop again.

Variation: You can line this afghan with matching fabric.

Bayadère Color Chart

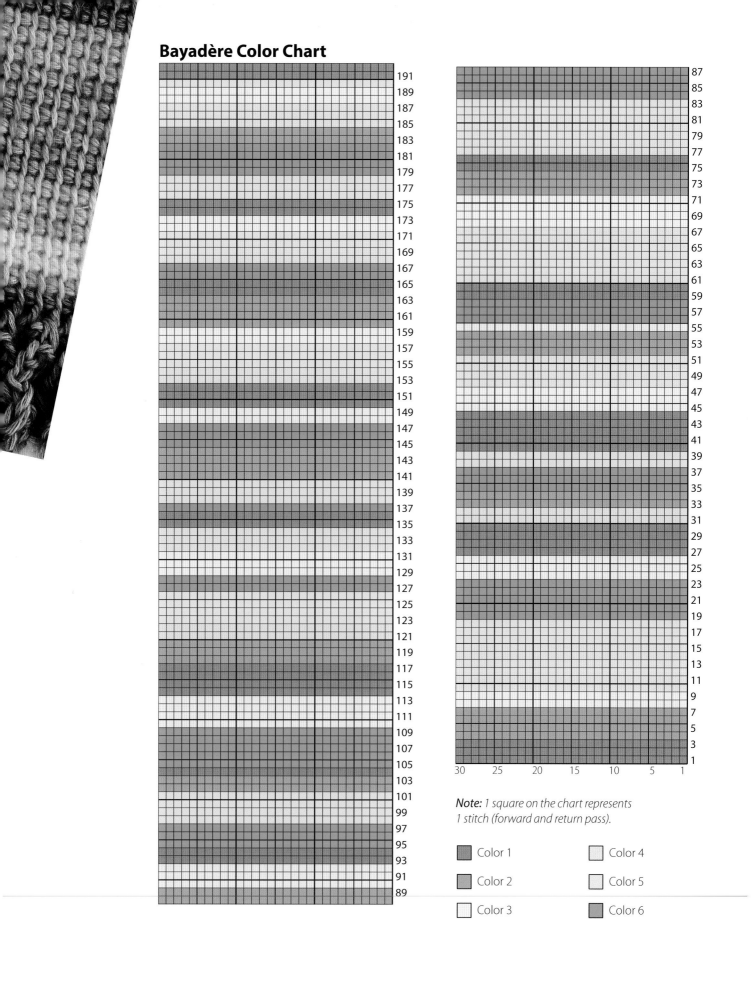

	191
	189
	187
	185
	183
	181
	179
	177
	175
	173
	171
	169
	167
	165
	163
	161
	159
	157
	155
	153
	151
	149
	147
	145
	143
	141
	139
	137
	135
	133
	131
	129
	127
	125
	123
	121
	119
	117
	115
	113
	111
	109
	107
	105
	103
	101
	99
	97
	95
	93
	91
	89

Note: 1 square on the chart represents 1 stitch (forward and return pass).

Color 1 Color 4

Color 2 Color 5

Color 3 Color 6

Little Poppies

Finished Measurements

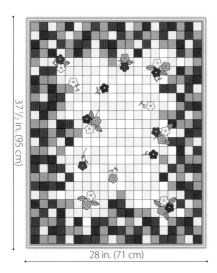

37½ in. (95 cm)

28 in. (71 cm)

Materials

- #1 super fine weight wool sock yarn in the following colors: 7 oz./200 g in each of white and ecru, 3.5 oz./ 100 g in each of yellow and light green, 1.75 oz./50 g in each of orange, rust, red, and dark green
- Crochet hook one size larger than what is recommended for the yarn

Stitches Used

Tunisian simple stitch, adding blocks diagonally (see page 9)

Chain (ch), slip stitch (Sl st), single crochet (sc), double crochet (dc) (see pages 4–5)

Half double crochet (hdc), treble crochet (tr), treble crochet 4 cluster (tr4cl), increase, increase with picot (see chart key on page 25)

Instructions

Note: This piece is constructed diagonally, from one corner to the opposite one. Since this project leaves a lot of ends, it's best to weave them in as you go, after finishing each block.

Work a foundation chain of 8 sts for Block 1. Work 6 rows of Tunisian simple stitch, then a finishing row. Fasten off. Add the other 500 blocks diagonally, changing color each time (for the colors, see the chart on page 24).

Little Poppies

Arrangement of the Blocks

310	329	347	364	380	395	410	423	435	446	456	465	473	480	486	491	495	498	500	501
290	309	328	346	363	379	394	409	422	434	445	455	464	472	479	485	490	494	497	499
270	289	308	327	345	362	378	393	408	421	433	444	454	463	471	478	484	489	493	496
250	269	288	307	326	344	361	377	392	407	420	432	443	453	462	470	477	483	488	492
230	249	268	287	306	325	343	360	376	391	406	419	431	442	452	461	469	476	482	487
210	229	248	267	286	305	324	342	359	375	390	405	418	430	441	451	460	468	475	481
190	209	228	247	266	285	304	323	341	358	374	389	403	417	429	440	450	459	467	474
171	189	208	227	246	265	284	303	322	340	357	373	388	402	416	428	439	449	458	466
153	170	188	207	226	245	264	283	302	321	339	356	372	387	401	415	427	438	448	457
136	152	169	187	206	225	244	263	282	301	320	338	355	371	386	400	414	426	437	447
120	135	151	168	186	205	224	243	262	281	300	319	337	354	370	385	399	413	425	436
105	119	134	150	167	185	204	223	242	261	280	299	318	336	353	369	384	398	412	424
91	104	118	133	149	166	184	203	222	241	260	279	298	317	335	352	368	383	397	411
78	90	103	117	132	148	165	183	202	221	240	259	278	297	316	334	351	367	382	396
66	77	89	102	116	131	147	164	182	201	220	239	258	277	296	315	333	350	366	381
55	65	76	88	101	115	130	146	163	181	200	219	238	257	276	295	314	332	349	365
45	54	64	75	87	100	114	129	145	162	180	199	218	237	256	275	294	313	331	348
36	44	53	63	74	86	99	113	128	144	161	179	198	217	236	255	274	293	312	330
28	35	43	52	62	73	85	98	112	127	143	160	178	197	216	235	254	273	292	311
21	27	34	42	51	61	72	84	97	111	126	142	159	177	196	215	234	253	272	291
15	20	26	33	41	50	60	71	83	96	110	125	141	158	176	195	214	233	252	271
10	14	19	25	32	40	49	59	70	82	95	109	124	140	157	175	194	213	232	251
6	9	13	18	24	31	39	48	58	69	81	94	108	123	139	156	174	193	212	231
3	5	8	12	17	23	30	38	47	57	68	80	93	107	122	138	155	173	192	211
1	2	4	7	11	16	22	29	37	46	56	67	79	92	106	121	137	154	172	191

- red
- orange
- ecru
- light green
- yellow
- white
- dark green
- rust

Edging

Join the light green yarn at a corner and work the 4 rounds shown in the diagram below. Work Rounds 1, 2, and 4 in light green and Round 3 in yellow.

Edging

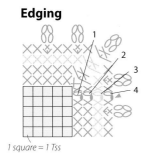

1 square = 1 Tss

(work Rnds 1, 2, and 4 in light green, work Rnd 3 in yellow)

Leaves

With light green, work a foundation chain of 9 sts, ch 1 to turn, then crochet 1 sc, *1 hdc, 1 dc, 3 tr, 1 dc, and 1 hdc*, work 3 sc in the next ch to go around to the other side of the chain, then return along the other side, repeating the stitches between the asterisks; finish with 1 sc and fasten off. Make 12 leaves in all.

Leaf

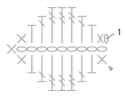

(make 12 in light green)

Finishing

Sew the leaves and the flowers to the afghan (see photo), then embroider the stems in backstitch, the little leaves in lazy daisy stitch, and the veins of the leaves in stem stitch, all in dark green.

Flowers

Begin with a ring of 8 chs, joined with a Sl st, and work the 2 rounds shown in the diagram below. Make 22 flowers total in yellow, red, orange, and rust.

Flower

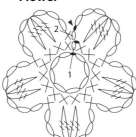

(make 22 total in red, orange, yellow, and rust)

◀ Fasten off.

◦ **Chain (ch):** Yarn over, draw the yarn through the loop on the hook.

● **Slip stitch (Sl st):** Insert the hook into a stitch, yarn over, and draw the yarn through the stitch and the loop on the hook.

✕ **Single crochet (sc):** Insert the hook into a stitch, yarn over and pull up a loop, yarn over and draw the yarn through all the loops on the hook.

T **Half double crochet (hdc):** Yarn over, then insert the hook into the stitch, yarn over and pull up a loop, then yarn over and pull through all the loops on the hook.

T **Double crochet (dc):** Yarn over, then insert the hook into the stitch, yarn over and pull up a loop, then work *yarn over, pull through 2 loops* twice.

T **Treble crochet (tr):** Yarn over twice, then insert the hook into the stitch, yarn over and pull up a loop, then work *yarn over, pull through 2 loops* three times.

Treble crochet 4 cluster (tr4cl): Work 2 incomplete treble crochets (leave the last loop on the hook) in the same stitch, then work 2 incomplete treble crochets in the next stitch; yarn over and pull the yarn through all 5 remaining loops at once.

✖ **Increase (inc):** Work 3 sc in the same stitch.

Increase with picot: Repeat 3 times in the same stitch: *sc, ch 4*.

Pom-Poms

Finished Measurements

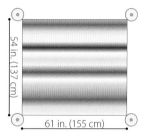

54 in. (137 cm)

61 in. (155 cm)

Materials

- Yarn of similar weight in 20 colors of your choice (here ranging from white to beige and from light gray to dark gray)
- Crochet hook one size larger than what is recommended for the yarn

Note: Don't hesitate to mix all kinds of fibers and textures in this project (cotton, wool, faux fur yarn, etc.).

Stitches Used

Tunisian simple stitch (see page 6)

Instructions

Sort the yarns by color family and shade. Begin with a foundation chain of 150 sts, about 61 in. (155 cm), and work in Tunisian simple stitch in a striped pattern as shown in the chart on page 28. Once all the stripes have been worked, the piece should measure about 54 in. (137 cm). If this is not the case, adjust the pattern by working more or fewer stripes. Don't work a finishing row. Fasten off and weave in the ends.

Note: To add stripes, randomly vary the number of rows per stripe and the colors used.

Finishing

Make 4 large pom-poms (see page 11) and sew them to the corners.

Pom-Poms

Pom-Poms Color Chart

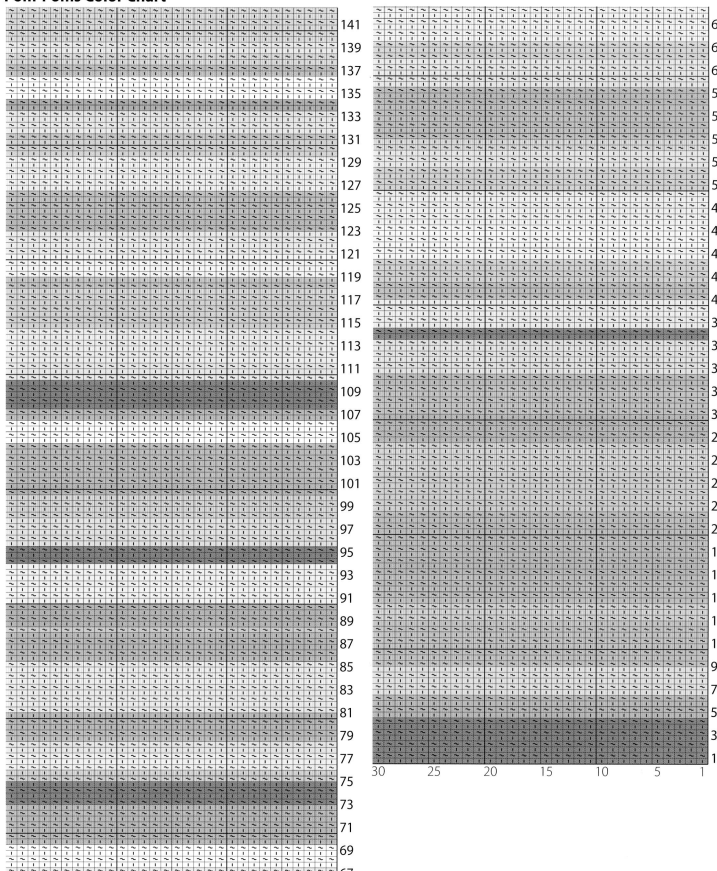

| Tunisian simple stitch (forward pass): Insert the hook behind 1 vertical bar, yarn over, and pull up a loop.

~ Return: Yarn over, pull through 1 loop, then repeat *yarn over, pull through 2 loops* across the row.

Color 1

Color 2

Color 3

Color 4

Color 5

Color 6

Color 7

Color 8

Color 9

Color 10

Color 11

Color 12

Color 13

Color 14

Color 15

Color 16

Color 17

Color 18

Color 19

Color 20

Botanical Garden

Finished Measurements

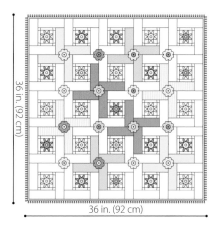

36 in. (92 cm)

36 in. (92 cm)

Materials

- #3 light weight yarn in the following colors: 14.1 oz./ 400 g in the main color (shown in white), 1.76 oz./ 50 g in each of 6 coordinating colors for the flowers, and 1.76 oz./50 g extra of one color for the edging (shown in DMC Woolly; 100% superwash merino wool; 1.76 oz./50 g, 136 yd./124.3 m per ball)
- Size E-4 (3.5 mm) Tunisian crochet hook (or one size larger than what is recommended for the yarn)
- Enough matching fabric to line the afghan

Stitches Used

Tunisian simple stitch (see page 6)

Chain (ch), slip stitch (Sl st), single crochet (sc), double crochet (dc) (see pages 4–5)

Treble crochet (tr), treble crochet 2 together (tr2tog), and treble crochet 4 cluster (tr4cl) (see chart key on page 32)

Instructions

Block

1. Start with a ring of 6 chs, joined with a Sl st, and work the 4 rounds of the motif (see step 1 of Making a Block).

2. Chain 10, and work Strip 1 (see step 2).

Making a Block

①

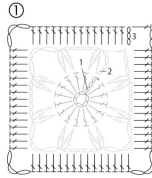

Work Rnd 1 in one coordinating color, Rnd 2 in another, and Rnd 3 of the motif in the main color (white).

②

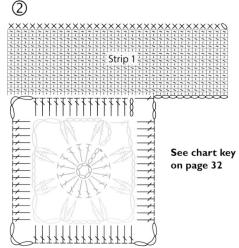

Strip 1

See chart key on page 32

For the strip, ch 10, then work *insert the hook in a stitch, yarn over, and pull up a loop* 29 times across the whole chain and the side of the motif block. You will have 30 loops on the hook. Return. Work 9 rows of Tunisian simple stitch, ending with 1 finishing row of sc.

Botanical Garden

③

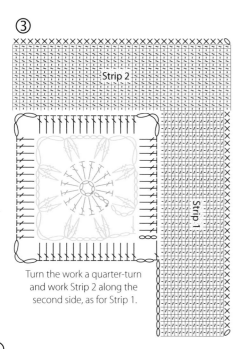

Turn the work a quarter-turn and work Strip 2 along the second side, as for Strip 1.

3. Turn the work a quarter-turn and work Strip 2 (see step 3).

4. Turn the work another quarter-turn and work Strip 3 (see step 4).

5. Turn the work one more quarter-turn and work Strip 4, but attach it to Strip 1 as you go, inserting the hook into the corresponding stitch in the chain for the last stitch of every forward pass and binding off the loops by 2 from the very beginning of each return pass. At the end of the finishing row (the sc row), join to the rest of the block with a Sl st in the last chain on Strip 1 and fasten off (see step 5).

④

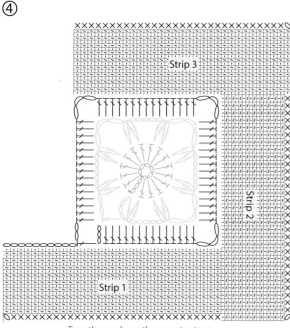

Turn the work another quarter-turn and work Strip 3 on the third side.

⑤

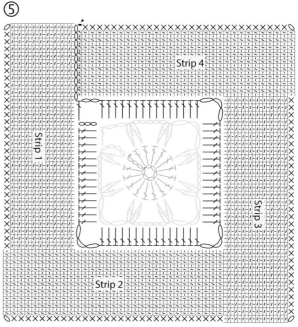

Turn the work a quarter-turn and work Strip 4 along the final side. Don't forget to join to Strip 1 as you go. End the last row with a Sl st in the last chain of the foundation chain of Strip 1, and fasten off.

◄ **Fasten off.**

○ **Chain (ch):** Yarn over, draw the yarn through the loop on the hook.

● **Slip stitch (Sl st):** Insert the hook into a stitch, yarn over, and draw the yarn through the stitch and the loop on the hook.

× **Single crochet (sc):** Insert the hook into a stitch, yarn over and pull up a loop, yarn over and draw the yarn through all the loops on the hook.

┬ **Double crochet (dc):** Yarn over, then insert the hook into the stitch, yarn over and pull up a loop, then work *yarn over, pull through 2 loops* twice.

Treble crochet 4 cluster (tr4cl): Work 2 incomplete treble crochets (yarn over twice, insert the hook into the stitch, yarn over and pull up a loop, then work *yarn over, pull through 2 loops* twice, leaving the last loop on the hook) in the same stitch, then work 2 incomplete treble crochets in the next stitch; yarn over and pull the yarn through all 5 remaining loops at once.

☐ **Tunisian simple stitch (forward pass):** Insert the hook behind the vertical bar, yarn over, and pull up a loop.

~ **Return:** Yarn over, draw through 1 loop, then repeat *yarn over, draw through 2 loops* across the row.

*~ **Assembly return:** Repeat *yarn over, draw through 2 loops* across the row.

↗ Insert the hook into the corresponding stitch of the neighboring block, yarn over, pull up a loop.

Make 25 blocks as shown in the diagram below, and sew them together.

Arrangement of the Blocks

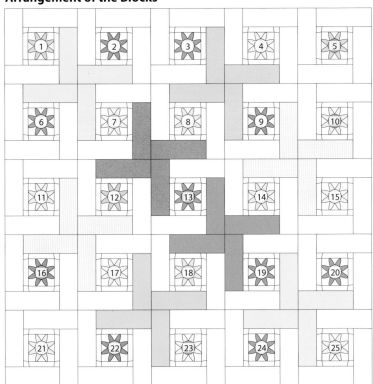

Border

With the extra yarn in one of the coordinating colors, work the 2 rounds of the border as shown in the diagram below. Fasten off and weave in the ends.

Border

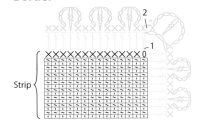

Strip

Flowers

Start with a ring of 6 chs, joined with a Sl st; work the 2 rounds of the flower as shown in the diagram below. Work each round in a different color (don't use the main color). Fasten off and weave in the ends. Make 16 flowers.

Flower

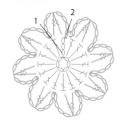

Work Rnd 1 in one coordinating color, and Rnd 2 in another.

Finishing

Sew the flowers to the afghan at the corners between blocks (see photo). Line the afghan.

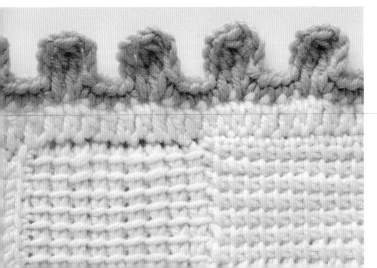

Pillows
and Rug

Flying Carpet

Finished Measurements

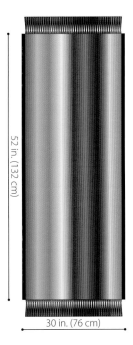

52 in. (132 cm)

30 in. (76 cm)

Note: This project is the simplest in the book; however, it's without a doubt the most expensive to make. One day, in a secondhand shop in France, I bought a collection of skeins of needlepoint yarn (that is to say, a whole cabinet full!). It took me a whole day to sort out the colors and set aside one skein of each shade. In all, I had 217 colors. To buy such a quantity of different yarns at a normal price would be quite expensive, but I still wanted to share this design with you in this book, because even with an everyday yarn and fewer colors, it can be very interesting to make. You could also take up a yarn collection: Ask some of your friends for several yards of yarn of a single thickness, and that's all there is to it!

Materials

- 100% wool yarn, 217 skeins of different colors but all the same thickness/weight (shown in DMC Colbert, 100% wool tapestry yarn)
- 5.29 oz./150 g wool and acrylic blend yarn in black (shown in Katia Merino Classic; 52% merino wool, 48% acrylic; 3 oz./100 g, 262 yd./240 m per ball)
- Size G-6 (4.0 mm) extra-long Tunisian crochet hook (or one size larger than the recommended size for the yarn)

Stitches Used

Tunisian simple stitch (see page 6)
Single crochet (sc) (see page 4)

Instructions

Start by sorting the yarn by color families (not necessarily from lightest to darkest) to obtain a gradient. Here, we move from blue to green, then yellow, then orange, then red, then pink, and finally mauve. As you work, select yarn randomly from each color family.

Work a foundation chain of 246 sts. Leaving a 4 in. (10 cm) tail of yarn at the beginning and end of each pass, work in Tunisian simple stitch, using a different color for each forward pass and each return pass. Make sure you have enough of each color to work a full pass. When only 3 skeins (lengths) of one color family remain, begin to work with one strand of yarn from the next color family at the same time as one from the current color family (i.e., work the forward pass in current color and return pass in new color or vice versa). This gives you a pretty, soft gradient between color families.

Once you have used all the different yarns, you should have 108 rows. However, this number can be changed depending on how many different colors you have and the desired size for your rug.

Finishing

With black, work a border of 15 rows of single crochet on the top and bottom edges of the rug (that is, on the finishing row and on the foundation chain). Fold each border in half toward the back and sew it in place with hidden stitches.

You can always weave in the ends if you want, but in this case you'd have to do it as you went—otherwise, you'd have 434 ends to hide! It's easier to make them into fringes. To do so, put them in groups of 5 and knot them together very close to the edge of the rug. Finally, trim all the fringes to the same length; for example, 2 in. (5 cm).

Bowl of Citrus Pillows

Finished Measurements

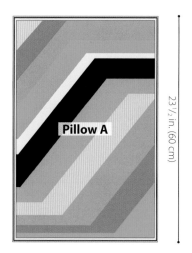

Pillow A

23 1/2 in. (60 cm)

15 3/4 in. (40 cm)

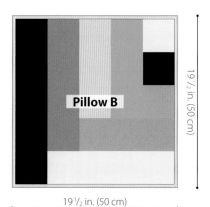

Pillow B

19 1/2 in. (50 cm)

19 1/2 in. (50 cm)

Materials

For each pillow

- 5.3 oz./150 g of #3 light weight yarn in each of 7 colors of your choice (6 for version C)
- Size H-8 (5.0 mm) Tunisian crochet hook (or one size larger than the recommended size for the yarn)
- Fabric for the pillow covers (see page 10)

Stitches Used

Tunisian simple stitch, adding blocks diagonally (see page 9)
Single crochet (sc) (see page 4)
Embroidery: running stitch

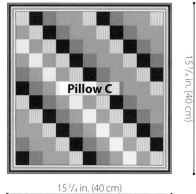

Pillow C

15 3/4 in. (40 cm)

15 3/4 in. (40 cm)

■ Color 1
■ Color 2
■ Color 3
■ Color 4
■ Color 5
■ Color 6
□ Color 7

|I| **Tunisian simple stitch (forward pass):** Insert the hook behind the vertical bar, yarn over, and pull up a loop.

|~| **Return:** Yarn over, draw through 1 loop, then repeat *yarn over, draw through 2 loops* across the row.

Color change: See instructions on page 40.

Pillow A

85
83
81
79
77
75
73
71
69
67
65
63
61
59
57
55
53
51
49
47
45
43
41
39
37
35
33
31
29
27
25
23
21
19
17
15
13
11
9
7
5
3
1

69   65   60   55   50   45   40   35   30   25   20   15   10   5   1

Bowl of Citrus Pillows

Note: *Don't cross the yarns over each other when you change colors. However, on the return pass, pull the two yarns through the stitch at the same time; this way, the two colors will automatically be joined together and you will not risk the yarn unraveling.*

Crochet a foundation chain of 69 sts in Color 1.

Work 2 rows of Tunisian simple stitch in this color.

Work 20 sts in Color 1, then work the remaining 49 sts in Color 2.

To change colors, work as follows: On the forward pass, work up to the stitch indicated, then hold the two strands of yarn as one and pull up a loop in the stitch. Then drop Color 1 and continue with Color 2 across the row. On the return pass, work in Color 2 up to the double loop, then work that stitch with Colors 1 and 2 held together, and then continue to the end in Color 1.

Change colors as shown in the chart (see page 39).

Finishing

Work 4 rnds of sc (work 3 sc in the corners) in the colors of your choice.

Make a fabric pillow cover (see page 10).

PILLOW B

With Color 1, crochet a foundation chain of 20 sts, totaling 4 in. (10 cm). (**Note**: *Adjust the number of chs if needed to obtain this length.*) Work in Tunisian simple stitch until the piece measures 19½ in. (50 cm) (Strip 1).

With Color 2, crochet a foundation chain of 80 sts (or 4 times the number of stitches in the foundation chain for Strip 1) and work in Tunisian simple stitch, attaching it to Strip 1 as you go as follows: On each forward pass, insert the hook into the first stitch of the corresponding row, and on each return pass begin right away with *yarn over, pull through 2 loops*. Work for 4 in. (10 cm) in Color 2.

For the following strips, pick up 20 sts (or the number of sts in the foundation chain for Strip 1) and assemble each strip to the previous ones as you go (see the arrangement of the strips on the opposite page).

Finishing

Work 2 rnds of sc (work 3 sc in each corner) in the colors of your choice.

Work a line of running stitch in a contrasting color along each joint between strips (see photo).

Make a fabric pillow cover (see page 10).

Pillow B

Arrangement of the strips

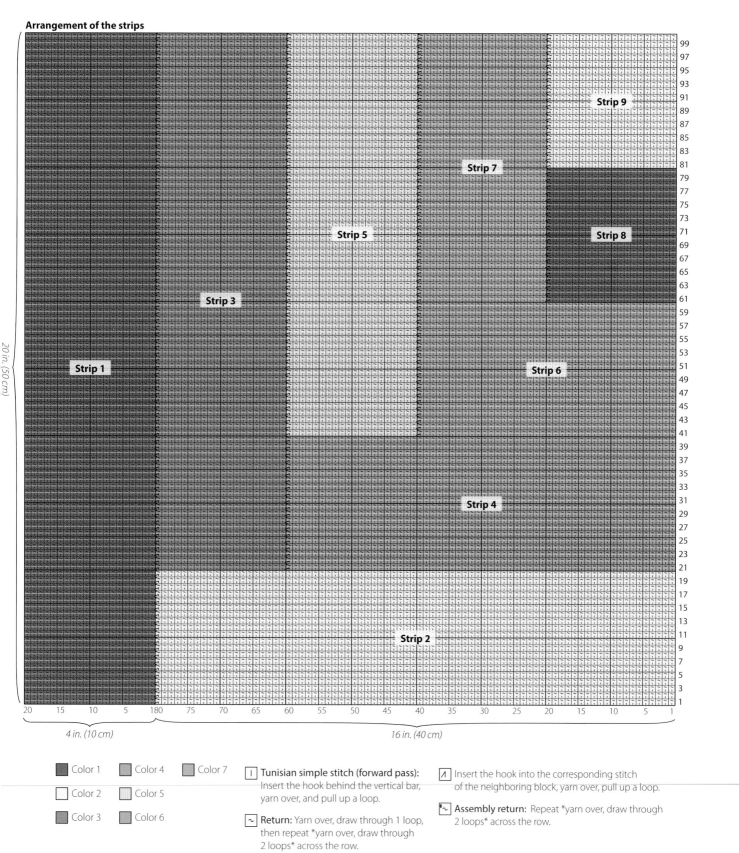

20 in. (50 cm)

4 in. (10 cm)   16 in. (40 cm)

Color 1   Color 4   Color 7

Color 2   Color 5

Color 3   Color 6

│ Tunisian simple stitch (forward pass): Insert the hook behind the vertical bar, yarn over, and pull up a loop.

~ Return: Yarn over, draw through 1 loop, then repeat *yarn over, draw through 2 loops* across the row.

⟋ Insert the hook into the corresponding stitch of the neighboring block, yarn over, pull up a loop.

*~ Assembly return: Repeat *yarn over, draw through 2 loops* across the row.

Bowl of Citrus Pillows

PILLOW C

Note: This project is constructed diagonally, from one corner to the opposite one (see page 9). Given the large number of ends in this project, it's best to weave them in as you go along, after completing each block.

Work a foundation chain of 8 sts for Block 1. Work 6 rows of Tunisian simple stitch, then 1 finishing row of sc. Fasten off. Then work the other blocks, alternating the colors as shown in the chart below.

Note: The bottom edge of the pillow should measure about 14 in. (36 cm); adjust the number of blocks if necessary.

Finishing

Work 6 rnds of sc (work 3 sc in each corner) around the border of the pillow, alternating between the colors of your choice.
Make a fabric pillow cover (see page 10).

Arrangement of the Blocks for Pillow C

Block 66	Block 76	Block 85	Block 93	Block 100	Block 106	Block 111	Block 115	Block 118	Block 120	Block 121
Block 55	Block 65	Block 75	Block 84	Block 92	Block 99	Block 105	Block 110	Block 114	Block 117	Block 119
Block 45	Block 54	Block 64	Block 74	Block 83	Block 91	Block 98	Block 104	Block 109	Block 113	Block 116
Block 36	Block 44	Block 53	Block 63	Block 73	Block 82	Block 90	Block 97	Block 103	Block 108	Block 112
Block 28	Block 35	Block 43	Block 52	Block 62	Block 72	Block 81	Block 89	Block 96	Block 102	Block 107
Block 21	Block 27	Block 34	Block 42	Block 51	Block 61	Block 71	Block 80	Block 88	Block 95	Block 101
Block 15	Block 20	Block 26	Block 33	Block 41	Block 50	Block 60	Block 70	Block 79	Block 87	Block 94
Block 10	Block 14	Block 19	Block 25	Block 32	Block 40	Block 49	Block 59	Block 69	Block 78	Block 86
Block 6	Block 9	Block 13	Block 18	Block 24	Block 31	Block 39	Block 48	Block 58	Block 68	Block 77
Block 3	Block 5	Block 8	Block 12	Block 17	Block 23	Block 30	Block 38	Block 47	Block 57	Block 67
Block 1	Block 2	Block 4	Block 7	Block 11	Block 16	Block 22	Block 29	Block 37	Block 46	Block 56

■ Color 1
□ Color 2
▨ Color 3
□ Color 4
□ Color 5
□ Color 6

Shawls and Scarves

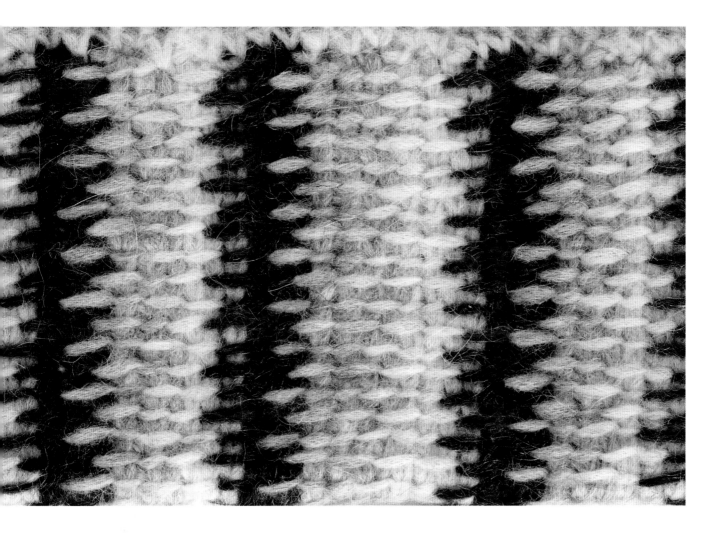

Frost

Finished Measurements

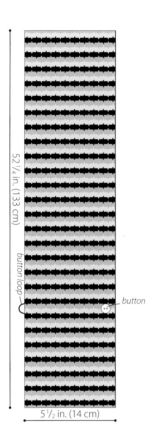

52 1/4 in. (133 cm)

button loop

button

5 1/2 in. (14 cm)

Materials

- 3.5 oz./100 g #3 light weight alpaca yarn in colors of your choice (shown in Lana Grossa Alta Moda Alpaca; 90% alpaca, 5% wool, 5% nylon; 1.76 oz./50 g, 153 yd./140 m per ball)
- Size J-10 (6.0 mm) crochet hook (or one size larger than the recommended size for the yarn)
- Matching button

Stitches Used

Tunisian simple stitch (see page 6)
Whimsy Stitch Pattern (see chart below)
Chain (ch) and single crochet (sc) (see page 4)

Instructions

Note: Crochet this scarf loosely. Since the pattern uses long stitches, the work has a tendency to get tight.

With Color 1, crochet a foundation chain of 43 sts, then work 1 row of Tunisian simple stitch. Continue in Whimsy Stitch Pattern (see chart). Repeat Rows 4–12 until the desired length is reached (about 26 times). End with a finishing row. Fasten off.

Whimsy Stitch and Stripe Patterns

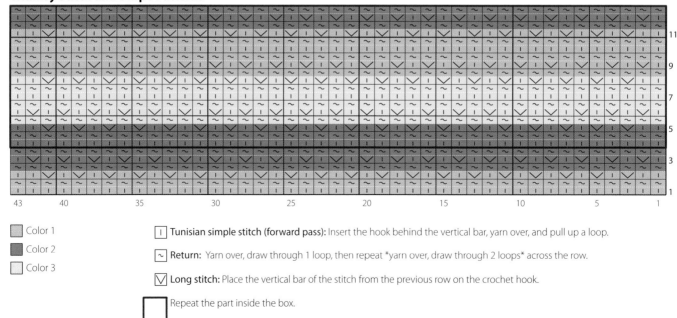

43   40   35   30   25   20   15   10   5   1

11
9
7
5
3
1

■ Color 1

■ Color 2

□ Color 3

|I| **Tunisian simple stitch (forward pass):** Insert the hook behind the vertical bar, yarn over, and pull up a loop.

|~| **Return:** Yarn over, draw through 1 loop, then repeat *yarn over, draw through 2 loops* across the row.

|∨| **Long stitch:** Place the vertical bar of the stitch from the previous row on the crochet hook.

☐ Repeat the part inside the box.

See page 74 for the instructions for the purse.

Frost

Finishing

Weave in all the ends.

Fold the scarf in half widthwise, wrong sides in, and attach the two long edges together with 1 row of single crochet, making sure the stripe pattern lines up.

Sew the button between the 7th and 8th black stripes (on the single crochet side of the scarf), and crochet a button loop of 6 chs with two strands of yarn opposite, on the fold side of the scarf.

Wintry Weather

Wintry Weather

Finished Measurements

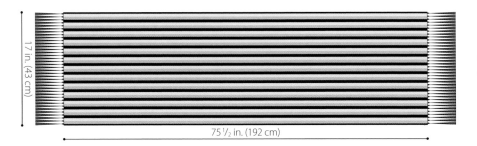

17 in. (43 cm)

75 1/2 in. (192 cm)

Note: *This scarf is equally attractive on the wrong side (page 49) as on the right side (page 51).*

Materials

- 3.5 oz./100 g #3 light weight alpaca yarn in each of 3 colors of your choice (shown in Lana Grossa Alta Moda Alpaca; 90% alpaca, 5% wool, 5% nylon; 1.76 oz./50 g, 153 yd./140 m per ball)
- Size J-10 (6.0 mm) Tunisian crochet hook, extra long (or one size larger than the recommended size for the yarn)

Stitches Used

Tunisian simple stitch (see page 6)

Instructions

With Color 1, work a foundation chain of 260 sts, then work in Tunisian simple stitch in the Stripe Pattern (see chart). After the 39th row, fasten off (do not work a finishing row).

Note: *Leave 7 3/4 in. (20 cm) of yarn at the beginning and end of the row on each color change. These tails will fill out the fringe.*

Finishing

Make bundles of fringe from 3 strands (1 in each color) of yarn 15 3/4 in. (40 cm) long. Use a crochet hook to attach them (see page 10) to either end of each row (78 fringes in all).

Stripe Pattern

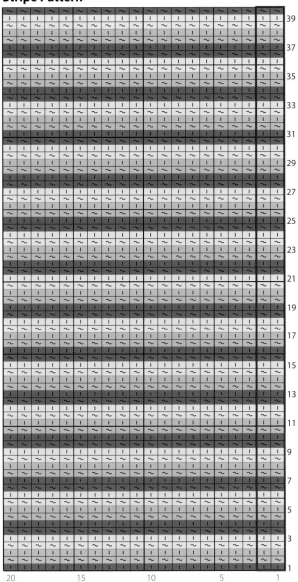

Color 1

Color 2

Color 3

| I | **Tunisian simple stitch (forward pass):** Insert the hook behind the vertical bar, yarn over, and pull up a loop.

| ~ | **Return:** Yarn over, draw through 1 loop, then repeat *yarn over, draw through 2 loops* across the row.

Repeat the part inside the box across the whole row.

Burlington

Finished Measurements

7 in. (18 cm)

55 in. (140 cm)

Materials

- 87½ yd./80 m #1 super fine weight wool yarn in each of 11 coordinating colors (shown in Rustic Wool Moire; 100% wool; 87½ yd./80 m per bobbin.) (**Note:** *This yarn is a bit stiff once crocheted, but simply washing the piece will make it more supple.*)
- Size C-2 (2.75 mm) crochet hook (or one size larger than the recommended size for the yarn)

Stitches Used

Tunisian simple stitch, adding blocks in a row (see page 7)
Chain (ch), slip stitch (Sl st), single crochet (sc), and double crochet (dc) (see pages 4–5)

Note: I chose the colors randomly for the sample scarf, but you could also order them in a pattern, as shown on page 54.

Chain 126 (adding a few extra, to be safe).

Work 9 blocks of 7 sts and 7 rows (including the finishing row) in a row in a single color.

For the next line of blocks, join a new color of yarn at the bottom right of the first block, chain 7, and work 9 blocks in a row, joining them to the blocks of the previous row as you go.

Instructions
Beginning of the Scarf

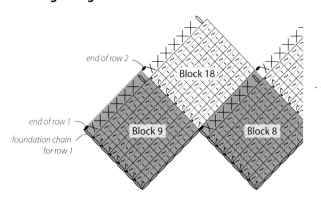

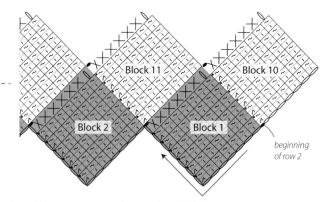

| | Tunisian simple stitch (forward pass): Insert the hook behind the vertical bar, yarn over, and pull up a loop.

~ Return: Yarn over, draw through 1 loop, then repeat *yarn over, draw through 2 loops* across the row.

⁄ Insert the hook into the corresponding stitch of the neighboring block, yarn over, pull up a loop.

~ Assembly return: Repeat *yarn over, draw through 2 loops* across the row.

○ Chain (ch): Yarn over, draw the yarn through the loop on the hook.

● Slip stitch (Sl st): Insert the hook into a stitch, yarn over, and draw the yarn through the stitch and the loop on the hook.

× Single crochet (sc): Insert the hook into a stitch, yarn over and pull up a loop, yarn over and draw the yarn through all the loops on the hook.

Burlington

Work the following rows in the same pattern, using one color for each row. Work until the scarf is the desired length (here, 50 rows).

This will yield a scarf with two angled ends, but straight edges.

Arrangement of the Colors

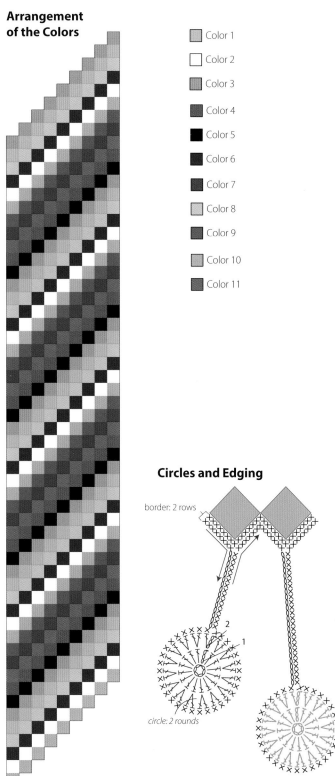

■ Color 1
□ Color 2
■ Color 3
■ Color 4
■ Color 5
■ Color 6
■ Color 7
■ Color 8
■ Color 9
■ Color 10
■ Color 11

Circles and Edging

border: 2 rows

2

1

circle: 2 rounds

Finishing

Circles (make 24)

Begin with a ring of 6 chs joined with a Sl st.

Rnd 1: Ch 3 (counts as 1st dc), then work 15 dc through the ring. Join to the beginning of the round with a Sl st in the 3rd ch of the beginning ch-3.

Rnd 2: Ch 3 (counts as 1st dc), dc in same st, then work 2 dc in each dc of the previous rnd. Join to the beginning of the round with a Sl st in the 3rd ch of the beginning ch-3. Fasten off.

Edging

Use the remaining yarn one color after another to create the edging, as follows.

Rnd 1: Join the yarn on the edge of the scarf, ch 1, and work 1 rnd of sc around the edge of the scarf (work 3 sc in each external angle). Join to the beginning of the round with 1 sc in the beginning ch-1.

Rnd 2: Ch 1, then repeat the following: *Work in sc to an external angle, work a chain (vary the number of chains from 15 to 25), take up a circle, sc in each stitch around the edge of the circle, then return in sc along the chain*, repeat from * to *, attaching two circles on the outermost corners of each end (as shown in the diagram on page 52), join with a Sl st. Fasten off and weave in the ends.

- ◌ **Chain (ch):** Yarn over, draw the yarn through the loop on the hook.

- ● **Slip stitch (Sl st):** Insert the hook into a stitch, yarn over, and draw the yarn through the stitch and the loop on the hook.

- × **Single crochet (sc):** Insert the hook into a stitch, yarn over and pull up a loop, yarn over and draw the yarn through all the loops on the hook.

- ╪ **Double crochet (dc):** Yarn over, then insert the hook into the stitch, yarn over and pull up a loop, then work *yarn over, pull through 2 loops* twice.

Mosaic

Mosaic

Finished Measurements

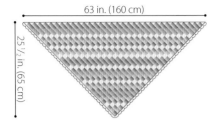

63 in. (160 cm)

25 1/2 in. (65 cm)

Materials

- 17.6 oz./500 g of sock yarn in gradient colors
- Size D-3 (3.25 mm) crochet hook (or one size larger than the recommended size for the yarn)

Stitches Used

Tunisian simple stitch, adding blocks diagonally (see page 9)

Chain (ch), slip stitch (Sl st), single crochet (sc), and double crochet (dc) (see pages 4–5)

Instructions

Work a foundation chain of 8 sts for Block 1, then work 7 rows of Tunisian simple stitch and 1 finishing row.

Be careful: The block formed must be a square; add or omit rows as needed to ensure this is the case. Fasten off.

Then add the other blocks and half-blocks diagonally (see Arrangement of the Blocks).

Arrangement of the Blocks

```
                                                                                        561
                                                                                   528  560
                                                                              496  527  559
                                                                         465  495  526  558
                                                                    435  464  494  525  557
                                                               406  434  463  493  524  556
                                                          378  405  433  462  492  523  555
                                                     351  377  404  432  461  491  522  554
                                                325  350  376  403  431  460  490  521  553
                                           300  324  349  375  402  430  459  489  520  552
                                      276  299  323  348  374  401  429  458  488  519  551
                                 253  275  298  322  347  373  400  428  457  487  518  550
                            231  252  274  297  321  346  372  399  427  456  486  517  549
                       210  230  251  273  296  320  345  371  398  426  455  485  516  548
                  190  209  229  250  272  295  319  344  370  397  425  454  484  515  547
             171  189  208  228  249  271  294  318  343  369  396  424  453  483  514  546
        153  170  188  207  227  248  270  293  317  342  368  395  423  452  482  513  545
   136  152  169  187  206  226  247  269  292  316  341  367  394  422  451  481  512  544
120  135  151  168  186  205  225  246  268  291  315  340  366  393  421  450  480  511  543
105  119  134  150  167  185  204  224  245  267  290  314  339  365  392  420  449  479  510  542
 91  104  118  133  149  166  184  203  223  244  266  289  313  338  364  391  419  448  478  509  541
 78   90  103  117  132  148  165  183  202  222  243  265  288  312  337  363  390  418  447  477  508  540
 66   77   89  102  116  131  147  164  182  201  221  242  264  287  311  336  362  389  417  446  476  507  539
 55   65   76   88  101  115  130  146  163  181  200  220  241  263  286  310  335  361  388  416  445  475  506  538
 45   54   64   75   87  100  114  129  145  162  180  199  219  240  262  285  309  334  360  387  415  444  474  505  537
 36   44   53   63   74   86   99  113  128  144  161  179  198  218  239  261  284  308  333  359  386  414  443  473  504  536
 28   35   43   52   62   73   85   98  112  127  143  160  178  197  217  238  260  283  307  332  358  385  413  442  472  503  535
 21   27   34   42   51   61   72   84   97  111  126  142  159  177  196  216  237  259  282  306  331  357  384  412  441  471  502  534
 15   20   26   33   41   50   60   71   83   96  110  125  141  158  176  195  215  236  258  281  305  330  356  383  411  440  470  501  533
 10   14   19   25   32   40   49   59   70   82   95  109  124  140  157  175  194  214  235  257  280  304  329  355  382  410  439  469  500  532
  6    9   13   18   24   31   39   48   58   69   81   94  108  123  139  156  174  193  213  234  256  279  303  328  354  381  409  438  468  499  531
  3    5    8   12   17   23   30   38   47   57   68   80   93  107  122  138  155  173  192  212  233  255  278  302  327  353  380  408  437  467  498  530
  1    2    4    7   11   16   22   29   37   46   56   67   79   92  106  121  137  154  172  191  211  232  254  277  301  326  352  379  407  436  466  497  529
```

To crochet the half-blocks: Attach the yarn to the bottom right of Block 497, ch 7, repeat the following 6 times: *Insert the hook in the stitch, yarn over, pull up a loop*, then insert the hook into the corresponding stitch of the previous block, yarn over, and pull up a loop. You will have 8 loops on the hook. On all the return passes, repeat *yarn over, pull through 2 loops* all the way across the row. On each forward pass, decrease as follows: Insert the hook behind the first 2 vertical bars, yarn over, and pull up a loop. Continue the row as normal. Work all the half-blocks in the same way. This will create a shawl with straight edges.

Half-Block Detail

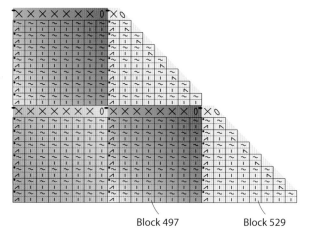

Block 497   Block 529

| I | Tunisian simple stitch (forward pass): Insert the hook behind the vertical bar, yarn over, and pull up a loop. |

| ~ | Return: Yarn over, draw through 1 loop, then repeat *yarn over, draw through 2 loops* across the row. |

| ⁄ | Insert the hook into the corresponding stitch of the neighboring block, yarn over, pull up a loop. |

| *~ | Assembly return: Repeat *yarn over, draw through 2 loops* across the row. |

| N | Decrease: Insert the hook behind the first and second vertical bars at the same time, yarn over, and pull up a loop through the 2 stitches. |

| ○ | Chain (ch): Yarn over, draw the yarn through the loop on the hook. |

| ● | Slip stitch (Sl st): Insert the hook into a stitch, yarn over, and draw the yarn through the stitch and the loop on the hook. |

| × | Single crochet (sc): Insert the hook into a stitch, yarn over and pull up a loop, yarn over and draw the yarn through all the loops on the hook. |

| ⊤ | Double crochet (dc): Yarn over, then insert the hook into the stitch, yarn over and pull up a loop, then work *yarn over, pull through 2 loops* twice. |

| ◀ | Fasten off. |

Finishing

For the edging, join the yarn and work the 5 rows shown in the Edging chart along the diagonal edges of the shawl.

Edging

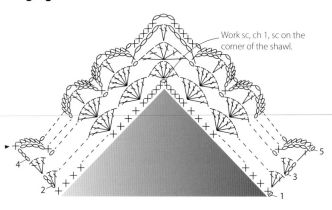

Work sc, ch 1, sc on the corner of the shawl.

Purses and Accessories

Practical and Stylish Tablet Cover, Pencil Case, and Makeup Bag

Finished Measurements

Tablet Cover

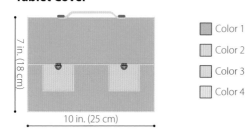

7 in. (18 cm)

10 in. (25 cm)

Color 1
Color 2
Color 3
Color 4

Pencil Case

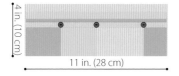

4 in. (10 cm)

11 in. (28 cm)

Makeup Bag

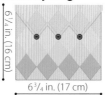

6¼ in. (16 cm)

6¾ in. (17 cm)

Materials (for the whole set)

- 1.76 oz./50 g #3 light weight cotton yarn in each of 4 coordinating colors
- Size G-6 (4.0 mm) Tunisian crochet hook (or one size larger than the recommended size for the yarn)
- 2 satchel-style clasps (for the Tablet Cover)
- 8 buttons ⅓ in. (1 cm) in diameter (2 for the Tablet Cover, 3 for the Makeup Bag, and 3 for the Pencil Case)
- 12 in. (30 cm) fusible web (for the Tablet Cover)
- Enough matching fabric to line the Tablet Cover

Stitches Used

Tunisian simple stitch (see page 6)
Crossed stitches (for the Pencil Case, see the chart key on page 63)
Chain (ch), single crochet (sc), slip stitch (Sl st) (see pages 4–5)

TABLET COVER

Note: Measure your tablet and adjust the dimensions of the case to match.

Body

With Color 1, work a foundation chain of 60 sts, about 10 in. (25 cm), and work in Tunisian simple stitch for 17¾ in. (45 cm). Fasten off.

With Color 3, work 1 round of sc (working 3 sc in each corner) around the edge of the piece. Fasten off and weave in the ends.

Pockets

With Color 3, begin with a foundation chain of 15 sts and work in Tunisian simple stitch for 2¾ in. (7 cm). Fasten off.

With Color 2, work 1 round of sc (working 3 sc in each corner) around the edge of the piece. Fasten off and weave in the ends.

Make two identical pockets.

Handle

With Color 2, begin with a foundation chain of 6 sts and work in Tunisian simple stitch for 5 in. (13 cm). Fasten off.

With Color 3, work 1 round of sc (working 3 sc in each corner) around the edge of the piece. Fasten off and weave in the ends.

Practical and Stylish Tablet Cover, Pencil Case, and Makeup Bag

Finishing the Tablet Cover

Sew the pockets to the front of the case around three edges (leave the top edges open) and sew the handle to the top using the buttons, as shown in the diagram below.

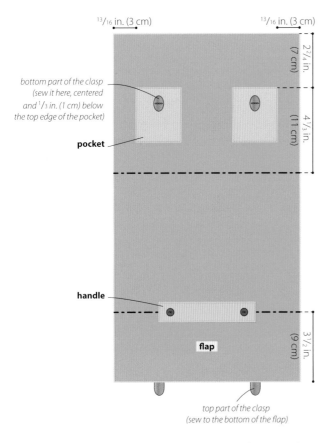

¹³/₁₆ in. (3 cm)   ¹³/₁₆ in. (3 cm)

2¾ in. (7 cm)

4⅓ in. (11 cm)

3½ in. (9 cm)

bottom part of the clasp (sew it here, centered and ⅓ in. (1 cm) below the top edge of the pocket)

pocket

handle

flap

top part of the clasp (sew to the bottom of the flap)

Measure the piece without the single crochet round.

Mark these dimensions on the fusible web and the lining fabric and cut out the pieces: Cut along the line for the fusible web and add a seam allowance to the fabric piece. Iron the fusible web to the wrong side of the fabric, then fold the seam allowance to the back and sew in place.

Sew the lining to the wrong side of the tablet case, just inside the row of single crochet (a border that stays visible).

Sew the side seams, counting the rows so that the case is even and lined up properly.

Center the bottom parts of the clasps on the pockets, ⅓ in. (1 cm) from the top edge, and attach them.

Attach the top parts of the clasps opposite the bottom parts, on the edge of the flap, making sure the case closes correctly.

PENCIL CASE

With Color 1, work a foundation chain of 60 sts, about 10 in. (25 cm). Continue by following the chart on page 63. After the 12th row, fasten off. This part will become the flap of the pencil case.

Continue in Tunisian simple stitch for the vertical strips. For Strip 1 (the leftmost one), with Color 1, pick up 15 sts (pick them up from right to left, as in any forward pass of Tunisian crochet), and work in Tunisian simple stitch for 5½ in. (14 cm). Fasten off.

For the following strips, continue in the same pattern, but join each strip to the previous one as you go (on forward passes, pick up the last stitch in the corresponding stitch of the previous strip, and on return passes, begin right away with *yarn over, pull through 2 loops* and repeat across the whole row). For the arrangement of colors in the strips, see the chart on page 63.

Finally, work 1 round of sc in Color 3 around the whole piece for the border (work 3 sc in each corner). Fasten off.

Finishing the Pencil Case

With Color 3, work across the top edge of the pencil case (the side with the horizontal stripes) as follows: 14 sc, ch 2, skip 2 sts, 13 sc, ch 2, skip 2 sts, 18 sc, ch 2, skip 2 sts, and finish with 9 sc. (**Note:** *The buttonholes should end up on the joints between the different vertical strips.*) Fasten off and weave in the ends.

Sew the side seams and sew the buttons to the front, over the joints between the vertical strips (see photo).

Variation: You can also line the pencil case (use the same method as for the Tablet Cover).

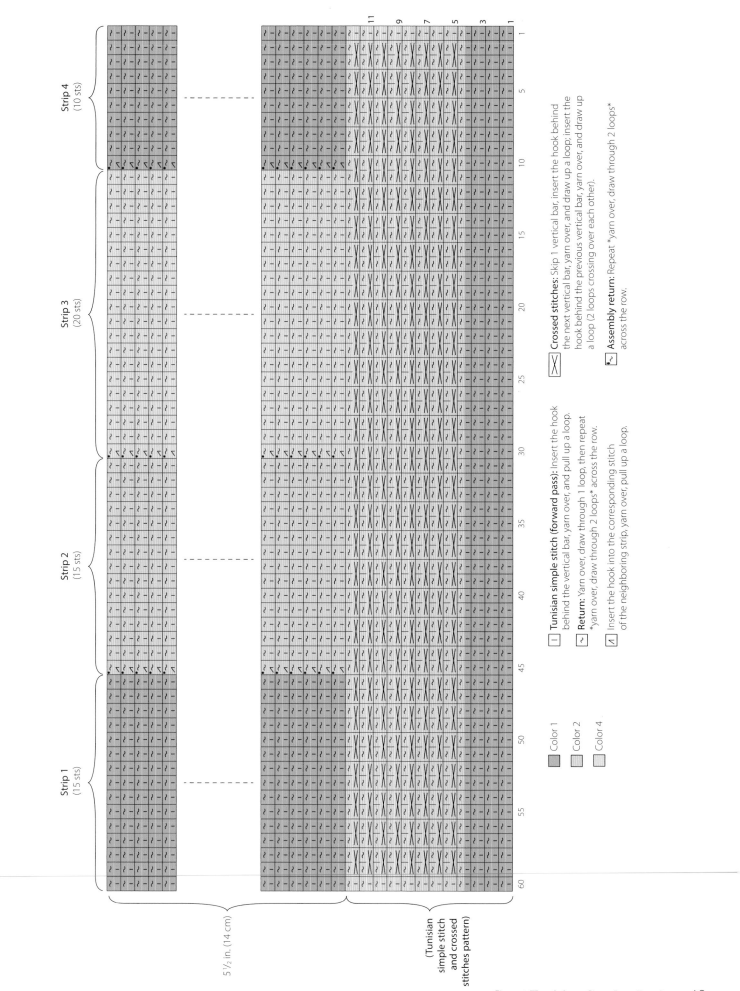

Strip 4
(10 sts)

Strip 3
(20 sts)

Strip 2
(15 sts)

Strip 1
(15 sts)

5 1/2 in. (14 cm)

(Tunisian
simple stitch
and crossed
stitches pattern)

☐ **Tunisian simple stitch (forward pass):** Insert the hook behind the vertical bar, yarn over, and pull up a loop.

➴ **Return:** Yarn over, draw through 1 loop, then repeat *yarn over, draw through 2 loops* across the row.

◹ Insert the hook into the corresponding stitch of the neighboring strip, yarn over, pull up a loop.

⨉ **Crossed stitches:** Skip 1 vertical bar, insert the hook behind the next vertical bar, yarn over, and draw up a loop; insert the hook behind the previous vertical bar, yarn over, and draw up a loop (2 loops crossing over each other).

➴ **Assembly return:** Repeat *yarn over, draw through 2 loops* across the row.

☐ Color 1
☐ Color 2
☐ Color 4

Practical and Stylish Tablet Cover, Pencil Case, and Makeup Bag

MAKEUP BAG

Each block consists of 8 sts and 7 rows (including the finishing row).

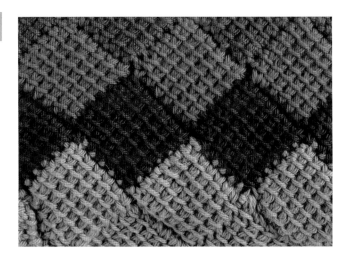

Body

With Color 3, start with a foundation chain of 120 sts (adding a few extra chs to be safe). Crochet 8 blocks in a row (see page 7), then join the piece into a ring with a Sl st (bring the two stars in the diagram together) and fasten off.

Tip: To make sure the blocks don't get twisted, fold the row of blocks in two, wrong sides together, before working the Sl st.

Beginning of the Body

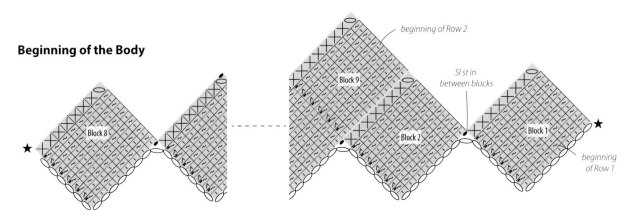

| | Tunisian simple stitch (forward pass): Insert the hook behind the vertical bar, yarn over, and pull up a loop.

~ Return: Yarn over, draw through 1 loop, then repeat *yarn over, draw through 2 loops* across the row.

⊿ Insert the hook into the corresponding stitch of the neighboring block, yarn over, pull up a loop.

*~ Assembly return: Repeat *yarn over, draw through 2 loops* across the row.

○ Chain (ch): Yarn over, draw the yarn through the loop on the hook.

● Slip stitch (Sl st): Insert the hook into a stitch, yarn over, and draw the yarn through the stitch and the loop on the hook.

× Single crochet (sc): Insert the hook into a stitch, yarn over and pull up a loop, yarn over and draw the yarn through all the loops on the hook.

With Color 1, join the yarn at the top corner of a block and work a new row of 8 blocks. Fasten off. Work a total of 6 rows of 8 blocks.

Next, work the **flap** as follows: Work 5 blocks in a row (make them so that, once the bag is assembled, the flap will match the back), then work 4 blocks in the next row, and finally in the last row (Row 9) work 3 blocks. With Color 2, work 1 round of sc around the top edge of the bag (ch 6 on each point of the flap to form 3 buttonholes).

Arrangement of the Blocks

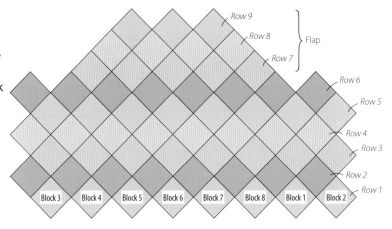

Practical and Stylish Tablet Cover, Pencil Case, and Makeup Bag

Finishing

For the bottom of the bag: Join the edge of Block 3 with that of Block 4, then join Block 4 to Block 5; on the other side, join Block 8 with Block 1 and Block 7. There will be 2 empty spaces left; crochet 2 extra blocks and sew them into these spaces to close up the bottom of the bag. Sew on the buttons.

Assembling the Bottom of the Bag

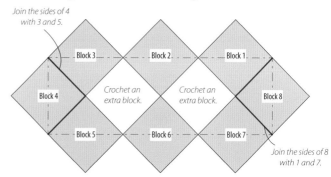

Rainbow Carryall

Rainbow Carryall

Finished Measurements

13³/₄ in. (35 cm)

18 in. (46 cm)

Materials

- 28 oz./800 g of #6 super bulky weight wool/acrylic blend yarn in the colorway of your choice (shown in Katia Inca; 53% wool, 47% acrylic; 3 oz./100 g, 109 yd./100 m per ball)
- Size M/N-13 (9.0 mm) crochet hook (**Note:** *Since there are very few stitches in each block, a traditional crochet hook is sufficient.*)
- 39¹/₃ in. (100 cm) stiff interfacing
- Enough matching fabric to create the lining
- 4 decorative buttons
- Stiff cardboard

Stitches Used

Tunisian simple stitch, adding blocks in a row (see page 7)
Chain (ch), slip stitch (Sl st), and single crochet (sc) (see page 4)

Instructions

Each block consists of 8 stitches and 8 rows (including the finishing row). Make sure the blocks are actually square; add or omit rows of Tunisian simple stitch if necessary.

Body

For the first row of 8 blocks, start with a foundation chain of 128 sts (add a few extra stitches to be safe). Work 8 blocks in a row, then join the row of blocks into a ring with a Sl st (bring the two black stars on the diagram together) and fasten off.

Tip: To make sure the blocks don't get twisted, fold the row of blocks in two, wrong sides together, before working the Sl st.

Beginning the Body

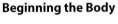

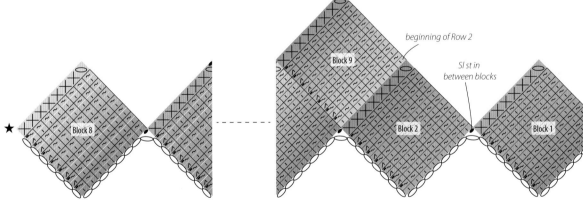

beginning of Row 2

Block 9

Sl st in between blocks

Block 8

Block 2

Block 1

beginning of Row 1

| | Tunisian simple stitch (forward pass): Insert the hook behind the vertical bar, yarn over, and pull up a loop.

~ | Return: Yarn over, draw through 1 loop, then repeat *yarn over, draw through 2 loops* across the row.

/ | Insert the hook into the corresponding stitch of the neighboring block, yarn over, pull up a loop.

*~ Assembly return: Repeat *yarn over, draw through 2 loops* across the row.

∘ Chain (ch): Yarn over, draw the yarn through the loop on the hook.

● Slip stitch (Sl st): Insert the hook into a stitch, yarn over, and draw the yarn through the stitch and the loop on the hook.

× Single crochet (sc): Insert the hook into a stitch, yarn over and pull up a loop, yarn over and draw the yarn through all the loops on the hook.

Join the yarn at the top of a block and work another row of 8 blocks. Fasten off. Work a total of 8 rows of 8 blocks. Work a row of sc around the top of the last row of blocks (working 3 sc in each corner). Fasten off.

Handles

Start with a foundation chain of 6 sts and work in sc for 19³/₄ in. (50 cm). Make a second handle identical to the first.

Finishing

For the bottom of the purse, join the edge of Block 3 to that of Block 4, then join the other edge of Block 4 to Block 5; on the other side, join Block 8 to Block 1 and Block 7. You will have 2 empty spaces left. Crochet two extra blocks in these spaces to fill in the bottom.

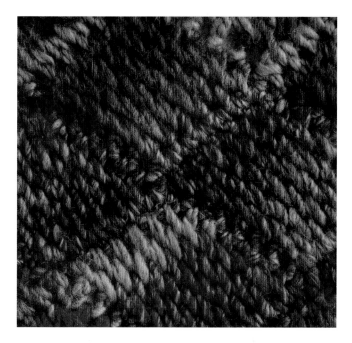

Assembling the Bottom of the Purse

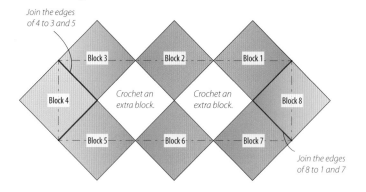

Join the edges of 4 to 3 and 5

Block 3 Block 2 Block 1

Block 4 *Crochet an extra block.* *Crochet an extra block.* Block 8

Block 5 Block 6 Block 7

Join the edges of 8 to 1 and 7

should now have the following reinforced pieces: 2 **a**, 2 **b**, and 1 **c**.

Join all the pieces together with zigzag stitch (if using a sewing machine) or herringbone stitch (if sewing by hand).

Place the lining inside the purse and sew it in place around the top edge with hidden stitches, going through all layers of the lining. Line the handles with fabric (to reinforce them), if desired, and sew them to the purse along with the buttons.

For the lining: Trace the back and front (**a**), the sides (**b**), and the bottom (**c**) of the purse onto the stiff cardboard. Cut out the pieces, then slip them inside the purse to check the measurements.

Back and front: Cut out piece **a** twice from the interfacing (without a seam allowance) and 4 times from the lining fabric (adding seam allowances).

Sides: Cut out piece **b** twice from the interfacing (without a seam allowance) and 4 times from the fabric (adding seam allowances).

Bottom: Cut out piece **c** once from the interfacing (without a seam allowance) and twice from the fabric (adding seam allowances).

Place 2 fabric **a** pieces together, right sides together, and sew around 3 sides. Turn right side out and iron. Slide an interfacing **a** piece inside, and close up the final side with hidden stitches. Do the same for the other pieces. You

Hues Handbag

Finished Measurements

13 ¾ in. (35 cm)

13 ¾ in. (35 cm)

Materials

- 10.5 oz./300 g of #5 super bulky weight wool/acrylic blend yarn in the colorway of your choice (shown in Katia Inca; 53% wool, 47% acrylic; 3 oz./100 g, 109 yd./ 100 m per ball)
- Size M/N-13 (9.0 mm) crochet hook
- Purchased handle 11¾ in. (30 cm) long
- Enough fabric to line the purse

Stitches Used

Tunisian simple stitch (see page 6)
Crossed stitches (see chart key)
Chain (ch), single crochet (sc), slip stitch (Sl st), and double crochet (dc) (see pages 4–5)

Instructions

Start with a foundation chain of 30 sts, which should be close to 10 in. (25 cm). If this is not the case, adjust the number of sts, making sure you still have an even number. Then crochet a 10 in. (25 cm) block in the stitch pattern, ending with a row of sc (see chart). Fasten off.

Crochet two more identical blocks.

Stitch Pattern

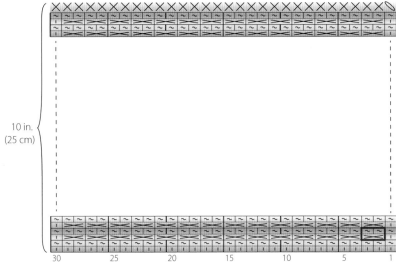

10 in. (25 cm)

| | Tunisian simple stitch (forward pass): Insert the hook behind the vertical bar, yarn over, and pull up a loop.

~ Return: Yarn over, draw through 1 loop, then repeat *yarn over, draw through 2 loops* across the row.

⋈ Crossed stitches: Skip 1 vertical bar, insert the hook behind the next vertical bar, yarn over, and draw up a loop; insert the hook behind the previous vertical bar, yarn over, and draw up a loop: 2 loops crossing over each other.

o Chain (ch): Yarn over, draw the yarn through the loop on the hook.

× Single crochet (sc): Insert the hook into a stitch, yarn over and pull up a loop, yarn over and draw the yarn through all the loops on the hook.

Repeat the part in the box across the row.

Hues Handbag

Finishing

Fold one of the blocks in half on the diagonal (bottom of purse).

Note: The diagonal determines the size of the bag. To find out what the diagonal of a square of a particular size will be, measure the side of the square, then do the following calculation: side x 1.4. Here, a side of 10 in. (25 cm) yields a diagonal of 14 in. (35.5 cm).

Fold the other two blocks in half along the diagonals and attach them on the left and right of the bottom, following the diagram below.

Assembly

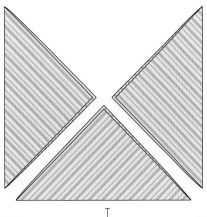

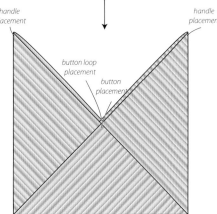

handle placement

handle placement

button loop placement

button placement

Work a round of sc around the opening of the purse.
For the lining, cut out 3 squares measuring 10 in. (25 cm) x 10 in. (25 cm), adding seam allowances. Sew them together following the same pattern as for the crocheted parts. Turn the lining inside out. Place the lining inside the bag and sew through both layers around the top edge using hidden stitches.

Sew the handle firmly to the corners of the bag (see photo).

Button

Leave a long tail after fastening off, then weave this tail through the last row to tighten it.

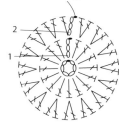

- ◦ **Chain (ch):** Yarn over, draw the yarn through the loop on the hook.
- ● **Slip stitch (Sl st):** Insert the hook into a stitch, yarn over, and draw the yarn through the stitch and the loop on the hook.
- ┬ **Double crochet (dc):** Yarn over, then insert the hook into the stitch, yarn over and pull up a loop, then work *yarn over, pull through 2 loops* twice.

For the button, start with a ring of 6 chs, joined with a Sl st, and work 2 rnds of dc as shown in the diagram. Fasten off, leaving a long tail. Use this tail to tighten the last round, then sew the button to the purse.

For the button loop, attach the yarn opposite the button and ch 12; attach the end of the chain to the purse with a Sl st, leaving a large enough loop for the button to pass through. Fasten off and weave in the ends.

Origami Pocketbook

Finished Measurements

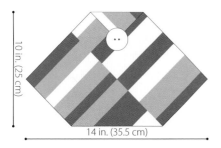

10 in. (25 cm)

14 in. (35.5 cm)

Materials

- 1.76 oz./50 g #3 light weight alpaca yarn in each of 3 colors of your choice (shown in Lana Grossa Alta Moda Alpaca; 90% alpaca, 5% wool, and 5% nylon; 1.76 oz./ 50 g, 153 yd./140 m per ball)
- Size J-10 (6.0 mm) Tunisian crochet hook (or one size larger than the recommended size for the yarn)
- Enough fabric to line the purse
- 20 in. (50 cm) of stiff interfacing
- 2 decorative buttons, 1½ in. (4 cm) in diameter
- 2 leather handles with clips

Stitches Used

Tunisian simple stitch, adding blocks diagonally (see page 9)
Chain (ch), slip stitch (Sl st), and single crochet (sc) (see page 4)

Instructions

Note: Each block must be square; if this is not the case, adjust the number of rows of Tunisian simple stitch.

For Block 1, work a chain of 24 sts, then work 16 rows of Tunisian simple stitch in the stripe pattern and a finishing row of sc. Fasten off. Then work the following blocks, joining them to the previous blocks as you go (see chart on page 77). Work 1 round of sc around the outside edge of the bag (working 3 sc in each exterior corner). Fasten off and weave in the ends.

Origami Pocketbook

Finishing

Join the edge of Block 5 with the edge of Block 8; do the same for Blocks 6 and 9, Blocks 3 and 6, and Blocks 2 and 5 (see the arrows in the chart on page 77).

Fold the points of Blocks 1 and 10 back onto the outside of the purse and sew them in place by sewing a button on each tip.

Sew the top edge on both sides along about half of a block (see the stars on the chart on page 77).

To make the lining, measure a block = square *a* (here, 5$\frac{1}{2}$ in. [14 cm] x 5$\frac{1}{2}$ in. [14 cm]).

Cut out square *a* 10 times from the fabric folded in half, right sides together, adding seam allowances.

Cut out square *b* (5$\frac{1}{3}$ in. [13.5 cm] x 5$\frac{1}{3}$ in. [13.5 cm]) from the interfacing.

Place two square *a*s together, right sides together, sew around 3 sides, turn right side out, and iron. Slide a square *b* inside and close up the opening with hidden stitches. Repeat the process to obtain 8 reinforced squares.

For the remaining squares *a* and *b*, cut one of the angles as shown below.

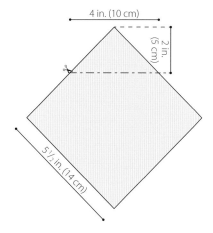

Sew and reinforce the angled squares as before.

Sew the squares together in the same arrangement as the crocheted blocks.

Note: The angled squares correspond to Blocks 1 and 10.

Sew the squares together with zigzag stitch using a sewing machine or, if this is not possible, sew the seams by hand using herringbone stitch.

Slide the lining inside the purse and sew the top edge of the lining in place with hidden stitches.

Use the clips to attach the handles.

Arrangement of the Blocks

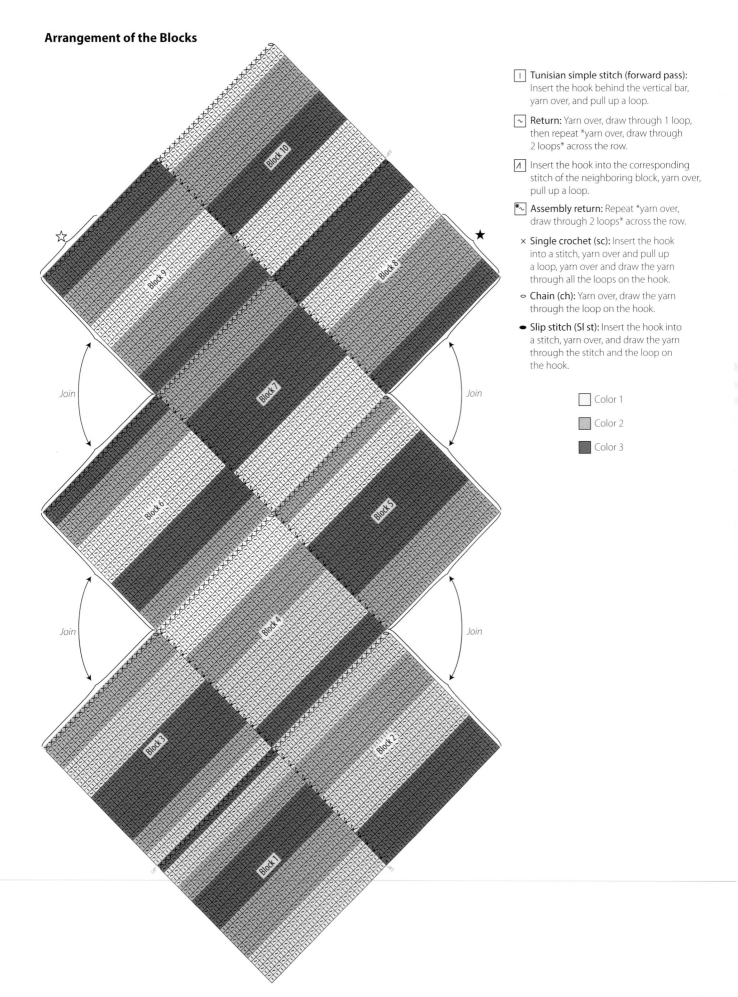

☐ **Tunisian simple stitch (forward pass):** Insert the hook behind the vertical bar, yarn over, and pull up a loop.

~ **Return:** Yarn over, draw through 1 loop, then repeat *yarn over, draw through 2 loops* across the row.

↗ Insert the hook into the corresponding stitch of the neighboring block, yarn over, pull up a loop.

*~ **Assembly return:** Repeat *yarn over, draw through 2 loops* across the row.

× **Single crochet (sc):** Insert the hook into a stitch, yarn over and pull up a loop, yarn over and draw the yarn through all the loops on the hook.

○ **Chain (ch):** Yarn over, draw the yarn through the loop on the hook.

● **Slip stitch (Sl st):** Insert the hook into a stitch, yarn over, and draw the yarn through the stitch and the loop on the hook.

☐ Color 1

☐ Color 2

☐ Color 3

Camel Belt

Finished Measurements

2¹/₃ in. (6 cm)

43¹/₃ in. (110 cm)

Materials

- 3.5 oz./100 g #6 super bulky weight cotton yarn in 2 contrasting colors of your choice (shown in Katia Cotton Cord; 100% cotton; 3.5 oz./100 g, 55 yd./50 m per ball)
- Size M/N-13 (9.0 mm) Tunisian crochet hook, extra long
- Belt buckle with a 2¹/₃ in. (6 cm) opening

Stitches Used

Tunisian simple stitch (see page 6)
Slip stitch (see page 4)
Striped crossed stitches pattern (see chart key)

Instructions

Start with a foundation chain of the desired waist size for the belt, plus 8 in. (20 cm). Here, we have a length of 43¹/₃ in. (110 cm). However, make sure you have an even number of chs.

Work in the striped crossed stitches pattern (see chart). Fasten off and weave in the ends.

Finishing

Fold the last ³/₄ in. (2 cm) of the belt around the central piece of the belt buckle and sew on the wrong side with hidden stitches.

Tip: This type of cotton yarn is made of three strands and is very thick. To make the sewing easier, separate the strands of the yarn and just use one of them to sew the belt to the buckle.

Striped Crossed Stitches Pattern

20   15   10   5   1

3

1

☐ Color 1
☐ Color 2

| Tunisian simple stitch (forward pass): Insert the hook behind the vertical bar, yarn over, and pull up a loop.

~ Return: Yarn over, draw through 1 loop, then repeat *yarn over, draw through 2 loops* across the row.

⋈ Crossed stitches: Skip 1 vertical bar, insert the hook behind the next vertical bar, yarn over, and draw up a loop; insert the hook behind the previous vertical bar, yarn over, and draw up a loop: 2 loops crossing over each other.

● Slip stitch (Sl st): Insert the hook into a stitch, yarn over, and draw the yarn through the stitch and the loop on the hook.

☐ Repeat the part in the box.

Originally published as *le Crochet tunisien*, Kristel Salgarollo
Copyright © Les Editions de Saxe—2015
www.edisaxe.com

Translation copyright © 2017 by
STACKPOLE BOOKS
An imprint of Globe Pequot
Distributed by NATIONAL BOOK NETWORK
800-462-6420
www.rowman.com

Printed in the United States of America

Designs: Kristel Salgarollo
Illustrations and technique instructions: Céline Cantat
Photos: Didier Barbecot
Pagination: Anne Roule and Tessa J. Sweigert
Cover design: Wendy A. Reynolds
Translation: Kathryn Fulton

British Library Cataloguing in Publication Information Available

Library of Congress Cataloging-in-Publication Data
ISBN 978-0-8117-1668-0